Delicious Book Design

Edited by
Megan van Staden

Delicious Book Design

images
Publishing

Contents

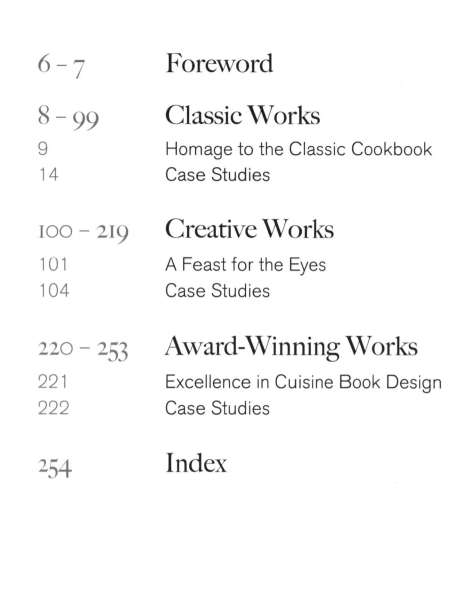

Foreword

Megan van Staden

It is no surprise that cookbooks are flourishing in this tough industry that is publishing. While the overall book market is diminishing, there seems to be an ongoing demand for useful and beautiful cookbooks. The emergence of food blogs and other readily available online information about cooking and healthy eating have fuelled a growing interest in this field, which has had a knock-on effect in the publishing industry.

Furthermore, blogging itself has resulted in the publication of many popular cookbooks, including *The Green Kitchen*, *Supperclub* and *My Daddy Cooks*. The author of cookbook *The Caker*, Jordan Rondel, is somewhat of a New Zealand celebrity, baking cakes for high-end fashion designers, as well as blogging and selling her cakes and books online. Indeed, to be successful within commercial publishing these days, authors often need a certain amount of 'following' created either through blogging, making TV appearances, creating/writing recipes for popular cafés and restaurants, or already being a celebrity chef.

Another factor in a cookbook's success is, without a doubt, its design. But what goes into the design process? The bones of a general cookbook include an introduction, then recipes followed by any additional condiment recipes, a glossary, and an index. These sections provide opportunities for the designer to create variations on their base design. Once the format, stock, and finishes have been decided, the designer will work within these constraints to set up their margins, select fonts and develop icons or hand-drawn elements.

The user-friendly, conventional cookbook layout design features a large title followed by an introduction, the number of serves, and cooking time. Ingredients usually fit into a narrow column on the left-hand side of the page, with a wider column on the right featuring the method. This is a space-efficient way to layout a cookbook, and is also visually balanced.

When paging through a book, a reader generally focuses their eyes on the recto (right-hand page), so publishers usually like images of dishes to sit on the right, so that they can be seen first. But nowadays, with designers pushing the envelope, there really are no rules, and some of the most beautiful cookbooks are the ones that go against the grain.

The structure of a book relies on the type of cookbook that's being published, as some books will be more technical, relying more on a rigid and alphabetical structure, and others more general and fluid, with recipes placed randomly throughout. These design decisions fall on the commissioning editor and author, who keep the target audience in mind, and provide the designer with opportunities to create different devices to signal chapters or breaks throughout the text.

Once the photography and styling have been chosen, and the author has a few sample recipes, the designer begins pulling together font and layout options. These decisions will be informed by mood boards created for the book, along with previously published works. The publisher and author will always have other books they'll put forward as examples of the genre; there will usually be at least one other author, book or iconic style that's the main inspiration and anchor point for the design.

Authors usually have their own special angle, or 'extra'. For example, *The Caker* uses high-quality organic ingredients and a few of the recipes are vegan. This attracts the growing population of health-conscious females who like to bake. *The Green Kitchen* is aimed at vegetarians and healthy folks, using lots of seasonal garden produce. Then there are the celebrity chefs like Jamie Oliver, who provides affordable, healthy, and flavorsome meals for people on budgets. Some books have the caloric information as a selling point, others cater for food intolerances and allergies, and many are heading in the direction of being healthy and organic.

It's the designer's job to tap into these key messages and visually communicate them in the best possible way. For a more organic and natural cookbook, the designer might use uncoated stocks, hand-drawn elements, and a natural color palette; for a high-end, degustation, hardback book, they might employ foiling on the cover, immaculate photography, and a clean and modern design. There are endless design elements and combinations.

The visual success of a cookbook depends heavily on all the elements of design, photography, styling and layout coming seamlessly together. That's why it's so important to solidify a concept from the beginning and to have a team of experts perfecting each part, similar to perfecting the mix of ingredients in a recipe.

This book features some of these successful cookbooks, beginning with a starter of traditional cookbooks, followed by a main course of creative ones, and finishing with a dessert of award-winning publications. We hope these help you gain more insight into the work and craftsmanship that goes into these useful tomes.

Classic Works

Homage to the Classic Cookbook

By Luca di Filippo

Defining the recipe for the 'perfect cookbook' is a very tough task. Cookbooks have evolved from mere recipe collections into publishing masterpieces, where food mastery merges with photography, food styling and design.

From a publishing point of view, everything started from the pragmatic need to keep a record and to sell the recipe manuals of famous chefs, but I prefer to imagine contemporary cookbooks as the advanced evolution of handwritten texts, typically scribbled on a little piece of paper, torn from a notepad and proudly collected in vintage metal boxes.

Design always takes into account marketing inputs and aesthetic trends. Nevertheless, keeping this sort of handwritten proto-cookbook in mind can help forge storytelling rich in emotions and enhance the reading experience.

Another crucial element that should interest anyone wanting to design timeless cookbooks is the role the internet plays in food culture these days. In our contemporary playground where, in just a few seconds, we can search for hundreds of recipes, how can traditional cookbooks compete? They can do this by maximizing the opportunity to involve all of the senses: paper quality and smell, inks, varnishes, tactility, size, weight and cover craftsmanship are, without a doubt, important purchasing motivations. Hence, approaching cookbook design as multilayered emotional storytelling, where all the elements are finely orchestrated, will help to achieve the ultimate goal: to sell the book.

Of course, there are many other factors at play that determine a book's success, such as exclusive content (not available on the Web), a chef's fame, marketing strategies and interesting topics. In the complex publishing industry, however, I believe that design should go further than just dealing with format and the arrangement of visual elements and typography. Therefore it's always good to team up with editors to create a balanced narrative where writing, photography, food styling, layout design, typography, binding and cover design come together to create a harmonious story.

For practical reasons I divide projects into two broad categories: brand-oriented and culture-oriented. Understanding which category your book falls into can help to better focus on the publisher's goals, organize the overall storytelling and define the criteria for design and photography style. Flexibility must always rule.

Typically, when a chef or a food company requires a (brand-oriented) cookbook, there's often an underlying marketing need. In these cases, branding knowledge will help to translate and merge the brand values in the publication, increasing the efficacy of the investment.

On the flip side, cookbooks dealing with geographical areas, ethnic groups or food typologies will certainly take advantage of a sociocultural and anthropological understanding in order to approach the project with an emphasis on research and discovery. This consequently creates the proper 'printed environment' for an emotional journey through different cultures.

Now, through an in-depth analysis of our selected classic cookbooks, we will focus on how to balance the four main design elements—Format and Layout; Photography and Food Styling; Typography and Typefaces; and Paper Quality and Finishes—to create captivating cookbooks that sell.

Format and Layout

Publishers' trim-size constraints and personal preferences from clients can often dictate what format a book should take. But when a project provides the freedom to choose the publication size and layout, I always feel it's like determining what came first: the chicken or the egg.

Format and layout represent the structure of a book, and I am always inspired by the approach architects take, where the functional aspect of a project informs its shape. In the same way, a book's content structure (it's not by chance we refer to the architecture discipline) will play an important role in defining both its size and layout design.

Typically, a good way to figure out the best solution for the 'architecture' of a book is to consider format and layout as one. Following—to avoid a long dissertation about such a complex topic—I focus on some key aspects of each.

• Format: Square Size

Anyone who has experience of publishing will know that printing costs represent a significant portion of the total cost of book production. In some instances, a landscape format could be very tempting to use, but budget and distribution considerations sometimes force designers to create layouts within a standard format, such as a square.

A square format (Figure 01) does have its benefits: it stands out from the crowd and is stylish and contemporary. This format also offers a very interesting option for linear sequences of images explaining a cooking process.

• Format: Portrait Size

This is the super classic (Figure 02). You can never go wrong with this format, especially if it's combined with a minimalistic layout. The austere and distinguished look will guarantee a neutral canvas where writing and photography will be the focal characters of the storytelling. I especially like this approach when the aesthetic qualities of dishes deserve the reader's whole attention and the written content merits no distractions whatsoever, leaving book lovers completely immersed in the narrative of the recipe.

• Layout: Brand-Oriented Approach

When fantastically executed, cookbooks about restaurants (Figure 03) can become the brand of their business. They are not only powerful marketing tools to boost brand

A1–A5. A meaningful sequence of images that either explains a process or adds dynamism to the visual storytelling
B. Text box positioning creates a graphic rhythm to the page
C. Functional margins aid readability

A. Clear and exhaustive recipe title
B. Centered ingredient list
C. Justified text to create a geometric box
D. Full-page image

A. Restaurant logo as focal cover element
B. Graphics from restaurant identity
C. Small white borders around pictures create a sophisticated layout typical of an art book

awareness, but also design pieces where brand values, culinary philosophies and unique selling propositions become tangible testimonials capable of communicating, to a very high level, the distinctive emotions embedded in the restaurant experience. Having a strong branding design background, I always suggest being consistent, consistent and consistent. Brand design, when properly implemented, offers all the guidelines for a coherent publication where constraints leave seemingly little room for creativity. In these cases, little details play a crucial role in defining the right tone and overall look and feel of a book, often carrying elements of the visual identity.

• Layout: Culture-Oriented Approach

Food is a keystone of any culture, a sort of magnifying glass capable of uncovering interesting details that allow us to better understand places, people and traditions. Building a content structure that captivates the reader through a tantalizing visual journey needs to be achieved, especially considering the amount of written text required in this kind of cookbook. This provides an opportunity to develop a layout where copywriting and photography find the perfect balance, depicting recipes and local mores. Often focusing on exotic countries or regions, a dual language layout (Figure 04) can often be of benefit—although this is a challenging task when a premium look and feel is required.

• Layout: Emotional Storytelling

This work (Figure 05) shows creativity at its peak. Its layout, typeface, food styling and photography are fused together to deliver a unique, warm output with a distinct homemade flavor. Orchestrating every single element to create a casual feeling and pleasant look is never an easy task. Like a personal notepad, this kind of cookbook communicates the human approach of chefs and writers, bridging the gap between professional chefs and food enthusiasts. Not only does it avoid scaring off newbie cooks with daunting food styling and a sophisticated layout, it also conveys an overall mood that welcomes readers to an approachable environment akin to a home kitchen.

Photography and Food Styling

It might sound obvious, but it is easy to underestimate the power of a well-coordinated project. A synergic effect is unleashed when all the specialists involved in a project—photographers, food stylists, designers—harmoniously come together, finely tuning all the visual elements to deliver a consistent product that maximizes the appeal of a chef's creations. This is especially so given that images make up more than half of a cookbook's content. It's an unmissable opportunity to produce images and layouts akin to an excellent orchestra playing with one accord.

• Fine Dining and Haute Cuisine

Anyone familiar with chefs will know how much they care about the final stage of their cooking creativity, reflected in their (often signature) plating. When dishes have

A. Area for image of raw ingredients
B1–B2. Color code to define two different languages or areas
C. Uncomplicated typography with highly readable typeface
D. Full-page image showing the final dish

A. Candid photography with food styling that looks natural and homemade
B. Image is used as background on the text page
C. Eroded typeface to add a casual look
D. Playing with misalignment to add dynamism to the page
E. Easily readable text when it comes to instructions

a strong aesthetic quality, a well-designed layout (Figure 06) lets the dish speak for itself. A harmonized graphic approach gives focus to the image while supporting the necessary instructions to prepare it. Here, the designer, chef, food stylist and photographer boosted the final result by collaborating to find the best choice of materials, composition, colors and photographic style. They remembered the golden rule—less is more.

• Homemade and Focus on People

Readers love a reportage style where details are the central part of the journey. Photography plays a key storytelling role in this kind of cookbook (Figure 07), and collaboration between photographers, food stylists and designers can help to generate the best layout to support the narrative. The homemade mood can be very useful in communicating a healthy and authentic way of cooking; this is a style that's chosen more and more by celebrity chefs, restaurants and chains. This trendy approach needs a very genuine and rich food styling, possibly made with objects found on location, combined with natural lighting and the presence of people.

Typography and Typefaces

There is an unquestionable need to magnify the aesthetic quality of dishes presented in cookbooks—not dissimilar to designing a museum or an exhibition for the display of 'food artwork.' The artist's statement becomes the chef's philosophy, and the artworks' descriptions, the recipe.

The style of the written text will help to define and modulate the quality of the environment: from a cool contemporary art gallery or austere historical museum to a folklore exhibition. Typography and typefaces represent the signage, and define the atmosphere that will immerse visitors.

• Neat and Tidy

I truly believe that 'less is more' should not become 'less is bore.' A clean minimalistic typography (Figure 08) has great potential to increase the perceived quality and high standards both of the chef's work and the cookbook itself. With meticulous attention to details, kerning, colors and typefaces, it is possible to transform a dull list into a design masterpiece where readability and aesthetic balance help readers during their cooking sessions.

• Speak Loudly

Typography is a form of art. Counterbalancing images with bold quotes or statements (Figure 09) can add an additional layer to a reader's experience. It is a very immediate and powerful way to set a specific tone of voice and graphic mood—the same sentence can change dramatically if a serif, sans-serif or handwritten typeface is chosen. In this way, typefaces can characterize the rapport we want to establish with an audience and creating a satisfying rhythm when flipping through the book's pages.

06

A. Consistent typography and elegant typeface
B. Use of color to highlight ingredients and create a distinctive look
C. Very pictorial food styling and vivid photography

07

A. Text box overlaying the image
B. Real people in their environment
C. Calligraphy typeface to enhance the human touch
D. Food styling rich in details and natural lighting

08

A. Clear title with sans-serif typeface
B. Tidy list of ingredients in a rigorous grid
C. Extremely readable layout for instructions

Paper Quality and Finishes

The tactile experience, combined with other design elements, is the main way printed cookbooks differentiate themselves from digital publishing. Is this another obvious point? I wouldn't say so. Quite often I flip through cookery publications that show no attention to paper quality, cover design and bookbinding, a precious craft and an art in itself.

Budget constraints are often a reason to cut expenses in the 'finishing department,' but I think missing this opportunity is a mistake that can affect the success of a publication in such a crowded and digital market. A designer's knack for problem solving and smart ideas may be of huge help to achieve the best compromise between tangible quality and production costs.

A. Full, handwritten typeface to make a statement
B. Tracing paper adds a sensory experience when readers leaf through the book

• Smooth and Warm

When a layout (Figure 10) emphasizes a homemade approach, graphic design elements can underline the casual tone, while photography and food styling can contribute to the depiction of a sophisticated yet natural daily life. Choosing an uncoated paper will add a tactile experience that reinforces this overall storytelling.

In any culture, rural environments represent an ideal place for organic, genuine and healthy foods; they're typically perceived as places where things are unadulterated by any unnecessary treatments, creating a warm, friendly and cozy ambience. In choosing an uncoated stock when selecting the materials for a book of this nature, a similar feeling is created for the reader.

• Vibrant and Accurate

With its hard glossy surface, coated paper makes the reproduction of photographs and graphics more vibrant. It is the perfect choice when a layout (Figure 11) includes images with delicate gradients and very detailed graphic elements, such as small icons, thin strokes or extra-light fonts. This approach is almost a must for a pastry chef's book, a section of the food industry where—very often—glossy surfaces characterize plated desserts.

Luca di Filippo is a creative director and photographer with extensive experience in branding. Lately, combining his great passion for cooking and photography, he is researching and developing innovative storytelling formats for the food and publishing industries. Based in London, he travels the world in search of inspiring tales and picturesque images.

Mainly
Mexican Menu

- **Designers**
  Mara M. Hernández Zepeda,
  Alejandra Sánchez Salas

- **Material**
  Black Geltex, 216gsm
  Cartulina Oxford Cambridge,
  160gsm Color Plus,
  150gsm Couche Matt

- **Printing Technology**
  Dry Etching

- **Size**
  215mm x 290mm

- **Completion**
  2014

- **Photo Credit**
  José Luis Castillo,
  Marc Fauche, Andrea Tejeda,
  Aintza Udaeta,
  José Luis Aranda,

'Mainly Mexican Menu' (*Menudo Menú Mexicano*), a compilation by media group Grupo Expansión, is dedicated to Mexican gastronomy. It is edited by Roberto Gutiérrez Durán and illustrated by Abraham García. The book has three stages: Roots of Flavor, which addresses the origins of Mexican gastronomy; Meal of the Day, a journey through modern Mexican cuisine; and Table Talk Dreams, culinary narrations of a Mexican foodie.

Mexico is rich in not only gastronomy but also culture, which is the inspiration for the book's design. Elements such as traditional embroidery, Talavera pottery, and patterns typically used in crafts are incorporated into the design, and many look as though they've been executed by hand.

The book's cover has a band around it that has been hand-embroidered, employing a traditional technique, and the section and recipe titles are hand-painted, which gives a warm and unique character to every page.

CALLE, MERCADO Y FONDAS

LA HISTORIA DE LA COCINA SE ESCRIBE TODOS LOS DÍAS EN el grito de una marchanta, en la destreza de un taquero frente a un trompo de pastor o en las cazuelas con arroz de nuestra fonda de confianza. "La hora de comer" es para millones de mexicanos el equivalente a dos tacos de guisado en el puesto de la esquina o a una comida corrida. Además de su rol nutricional, estos espacios son un punto de encuentro heterogéneo que no hace distinciones de creencias ni de clase social. La calle, el mercado y la fonda son la base de un complejo tejido cultural que nutre a diario nuestros apetitos y nuestra rica identidad.

EL TACO
Y LA PLAZA

POR MARIANA CAMACHO # FOTOS JOSÉ LUIS CASTILLO
MONTA: AIRE

Tijuana es un punto neurálgico en materia de cocina callejera. Una ciudad fronteriza, donde la tortilla arropa el eclecticismo. Hogar de los tacos de asada, de las carretas de mariscos y de las mil y un salsas.

E n una de sus visitas a México entrevisté a Rick Bayless (chef propietario de varios restaurantes de cocina mexicana en Chicago, como Frontera Grill) acerca de los destinos de México que más han influido en su cocina. Sin pensarlo mucho me dijo "Oaxaca" y luego sonrió, y agregó a la lista: Tijuana. "Siempre pensé que el DF tenía los mejores tacos, pero hace poco hice un viaje a Tijuana y cambié de opinión".

Tiene razón, la cocina de las calles de Tijuana es emocionante, por los tacos, sí, al igual que por las tortas y las salsas. ¿Qué tienen de especial? Pensándolo muy bien, diría que son las salsas. Las tortas de Wash (Av. Jalisco s/n, el Cacho), por ejemplo, tienen muy buena telera y muy buena carne asada, pero el guacamole y la salsa roja se cocinan aparte. Después, en las mesas del Food Garden –un proyecto con varios

PÁGINA OPUESTA
Uno de los tacos "estilo Tijuana" de Kokopelli.

UNA COMIDA PERFECTA

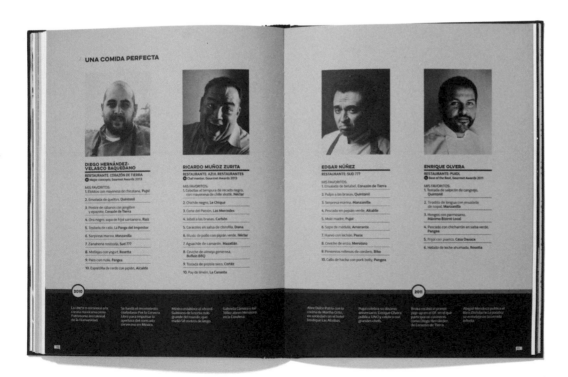

DIEGO HERNÁNDEZ-VELASCO BAQUEDANO
RESTAURANTE: CORAZÓN DE TIERRA
Mejor concepto, Gourmet Awards 2013

MIS FAVORITOS:
1. Elotitos con mayonesa de chicatana, **Pujol**
2. Ensalada de quelites, **Quintonil**
3. Postre de rábanos con jengibre y epazote, **Corazón de Tierra**
4. Oro negro, sopa de frijol santanero, **Raíz**
5. Tostada de callo, **La Panga del Impostor**
6. Sorpresa marina, **Manzanilla**
7. Zanahoria rostizada, **Sud 777**
8. Molitegas con yogurt, **Rosetta**
9. Pato con mole, **Pangea**
10. Espaldilla de cerdo con pipián, **Alcalde**

RICARDO MUÑOZ ZURITA
RESTAURANTE: AZUL RESTAURANTES
Chef mentor, Gourmet Awards 2013

MIS FAVORITOS:
1. Cebollas el tempura de recado negro, con mayonesa de chile skalla, **Néctar**
2. Chichilo negro, **Le Chique**
3. Corte del Patrón, **Las Mercedes**
4. Pescado en pepián verde, **Alcalde**
5. Jabalí a las brasas, **Carbón**
6. Caracoles en salsa de clorofila, **Diana**
7. Muslo de pollo con pipián verde, **Néctar**
8. Aguachile de camarón, **Mazatlán**
9. Tostada de pozole seco, **Cortés**
10. Pay de limón, **La Canasta**

EDGAR NÚÑEZ
RESTAURANTE: SUD 777

MIS FAVORITOS:
1. Ensalada de betabel, **Corazón de Tierra**
2. Pulpo a las brasas, **Quintonil**
3. Sorpresa marina, **Manzanilla**
4. Pescado en pepián verde, **Alcalde**
5. Mole madre, **Pujol**
6. Sopa de médula, **Amaranta**
7. Huevo con lechón, **Pasta**
8. Ceviche de erizo, **Merotoro**
9. Pimientos rellenos de cordero, **Biko**
10. Callo de hacha con pork belly, **Pangea**

ENRIQUE OLVERA
RESTAURANTE: PUJOL
Best of the Best, Gourmet Awards 2011

MIS FAVORITOS:
1. Tostada de salpicón de cangrejo, **Quintonil**
2. Tiradito de lengua con ensalada de nopal, **Manzanilla**
3. Hongos con parmesano, **Máximo Bistrot Local**
4. Pescado con chicharrón en salsa verde, **Pangea**
5. Frijol con puerco, **Casa Oaxaca**
6. Helado de leche ahumada, **Rosetta**

2010

2011

16

4 CHARANDA

5 CAFÉ

EN PROCESO DE OBTENER DENOMINACIÓN DE ORIGEN.

Vainilla de Papantla

Chile habanero

VERACRUZ

CHIAPAS

MARCAS COLECTIVAS

QUESO COTIJA

TLAYUDAS MI QUERENCIA

DE VUELTA A LO NATURAL

EL COCINERO MODERNO

ATRÁS QUEDARON LOS DÍAS EN LOS QUE LOS COCINEROS tenían como principal tarea el entregarse a la sazón de sus guisos. Hoy, el oficio demanda otras habilidades. Para ser chef hay que tener mucho apetito, hambre para viajar, buen ojo para reconocer e interpretar una tendencia y tacto para dialogar con la gastronomía tradicional. Tiene que ser bueno en los fogones, en las redes sociales, en las relaciones públicas y en los negocios. Además, en la búsqueda de los mejores productos, hacer todo lo que esté en sus manos para disminuir su huella ambiental. El cocinero moderno es el nuevo renacentista, un todólogo entregado al servicio de sus comensales y a la buena comida.

MEMORIAS DE UNA FOODIE

This 560-page cookbook captures the life of The Engine Room—a highly awarded New Zealand eatery. It includes over 2000 images, capturing the restaurant's inner workings, as well as 100-plus recipes. The design brief was to express the honest values and passion of the restaurant.

Some key graphic elements are used in the book, which were inspired by the restaurant itself. Daily menus are written on a blackboard by the chefs, and this is graphically represented on the book's front cover, which uses black paper with white ink. The silver foil logo references the chrome of the restaurant's signage and enamel pins worn by the staff. All photos of the recipes were shot on craft stock, to reinforce the bistro's community feel, and the craft paper aesthetic was also used on the case binding.

This is a cookbook that's designed to really cook with—the font size of the recipe text is large to aid readability, ingredients are pulled out using the color blue and the layout is straightforward and practical.

The Engine Room

- **Design Agency**
  Alt Group

- **Designer**
  Dean Poole

- **Printing Technology**
  Silver Hot Foil Stamp,
  White Foil Stamp

- **Size**
  260mm x 200mm

- **Completion**
  2013

- **Photo Credit**
  Toaki Okano

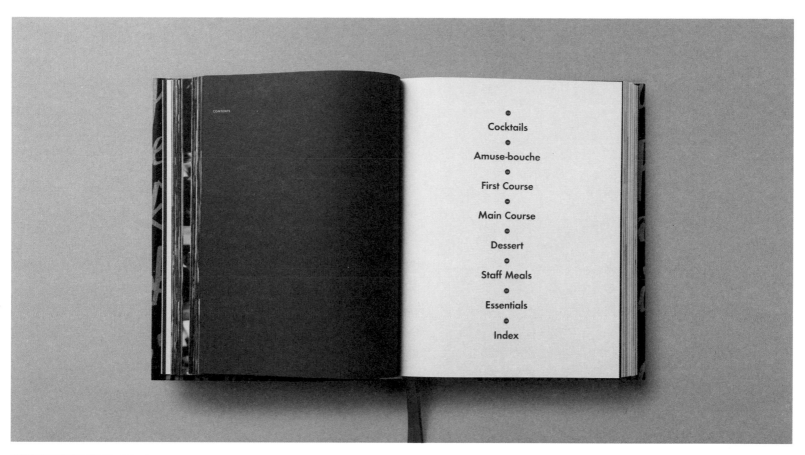

CONTENTS

OYSTERS
MIGNONETTE
P.155

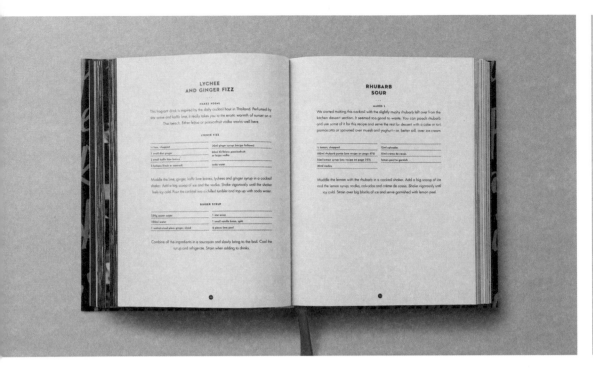

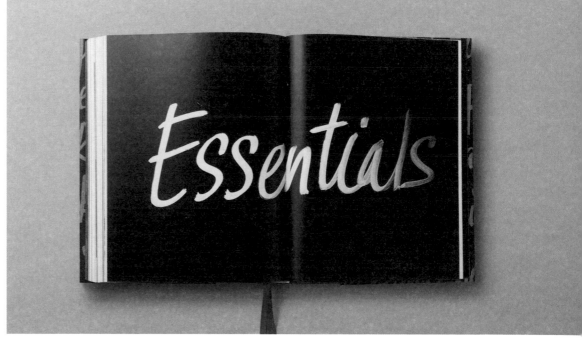

70 Favourite Recipes

- **Designer**
  Bianca Wolmerans

- **Material**
  240gsm and 100gsm Munken Polar

- **Printing Technology**
  UV Varnish

- **Size**
  210mm x 270mm

- **Completion**
  2014

- **Photo Credit**
  Bianca Wolmerans, Bluegraphic

Bianca Wolmerans came up with the idea for this book after her uncle, who loves cooking and has spent many years spoiling Bianca's family with wonderful meals, recently turned 70. She wanted to create something that would show her appreciation for her uncle's cooking and inspire others to come up with their own delights in the kitchen.

Bianca, who is also the designer of the book, asked 70 of her uncle's friends and relatives to provide their one favorite recipe, and these were compiled into this book, accompanied by messages of love and friendship. The cooking of the recipes, food styling and photography took place at Bianca's home; her parents prepared the meals while she handled the entire creative element to create this very special gift made with love.

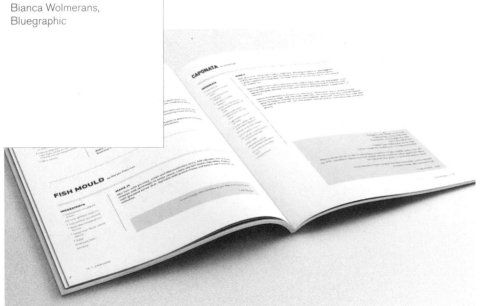

SPINASIETERT by Marianne Wessels

INGREDIENTS

Kors

Gekoopte skilferkors

Vulsel

1 pakkie wit of bruin
   uiesoppoeier

250ml suurroom

1 ui, gekap

500g vars spinasie

10 ml sonneblom olie

1 houer(250g) fyn maaskaas

3 eiers, goed geklits

sout, peper en mostert na
   smaak

100g(250ml) gerasperde
   Cheddar kaas

MAKE IT

Verhit die oond tot 190˚C

Voer tertbord met deeg uit. Meng die soppoeier en suurroom en laat dit 15 min lank
staan. Was die spinasie en plaas die nat blare in 'n groot kastrol. Sit die deksel op
en stoom oor matige hitte net tot sag sonder om ekstra vloeistof by te voeg. Haal
die blare uit, sny die stingelgedeeltes uit en snipper die res fyn. Soteer die ui in die
olie en meng met die spinasie. Voeg die maaskaas, eiers, sopmengsel, sout, peper,
mostert en 2/3 van kaas by. Meng goed.

Skep vulsel in rou kors, strooi die oorblywende kaas bo-oor en bak vir 35 tot 40 min.

Baie voorspoedige 70ste verjaarsdag. Mag dit 'n wonderlike jaar wees.

Baie liefde,
Mariana en John

GREEN BEANS WITH PEARS & BACON

BROCCOLI & CAULIFLOWER SALAD

HONEY PRAWNS

GARLIC BUTTER CRAYFISH

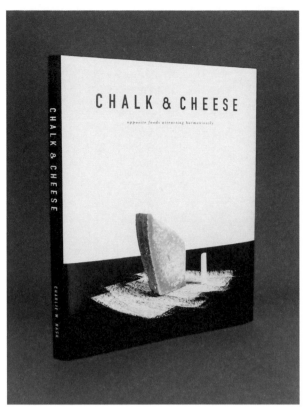

Chalk & Cheese

- **Designer**
  Charlie W. Nash

- **Material**
  120gsm Cranes Crest
  White—GF Smith

- **Size**
  220mm x 270mm

- **Completion**
  2015

This book consists of a selection of recipes that include ingredients that are opposite either visually or in taste. The aim of the book is to explain how certain foods go together, and to open readers' minds to the art of food pairing. This is especially so in instances where our preconceptions tell us that certain foods should not be paired together.

Each recipe's layout has been carefully crafted to ensure readers do not establish such preconceptions beforehand. The photographic style throughout the book is highly appetizing and repeatedly reinforces the idea that opposites attract.

A major visual aesthetic throughout the book is a slash symbol, used to split and attract the ingredients. Circles are another repeated design element, representing either a single ingredient or, when conjoined, ingredients that have been consolidated. The book's designer, Charlie W. Nash, also created an ampersand symbol to visually coincide with the conjoining circles. Many of the spreads feature a unique chalk mark to support the 'Chalk & Cheese' theme.

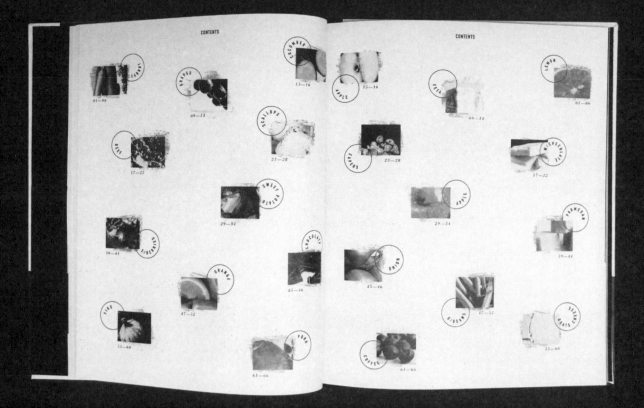

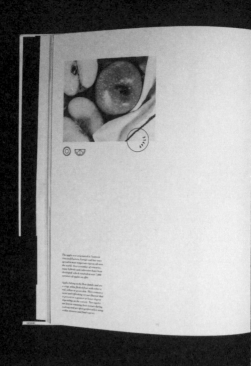

SWEET POTATO & APPLE

GRAPES & FETA

For the grapes

For the feta

To Serve

	For 2	For 6	For 10

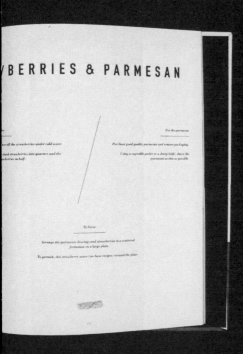

...BERRIES & PARMESAN

For the parmesan

To Serve

This is a cookbook about preserving food. Recipes are brought to life with photography that captures the homemade and wholesome aspects of preserving, and reveals the sensual nature of the food. The use of fabric for the cover extends this tactile, homespun concept, while the inclusion of uncoated paper emphasizes the natural and raw.

The result is a book that is as artistic as it is useful, something that can be enjoyed as an art object as well as a source of great recipes and fascinating stories about the preserving industry. The result is so evocative that the reader can almost taste the food.

What's Old is New Again

- **Design Agency**
  Watts Design

- **Designer**
  Helen Watts

- **Material**
  Jacket: 125gsm Duralin, 3mm Muda Chipboard, FSC 100 percent RC Graphic Board; Text: 170gsm Tauro Wood-Free

- **Printing Technology**
  Embossing, Matt Varnish, White Foil Stamping

- **Size**
  240mm x 250mm

- **Completion**
  2015

- **Photo Credit**
  James Vlahogiannis

Luscious

- **Designer**
  Ewelina Bocian

- **Size**
  210mm x 280mm

- **Completion**
  2012

- **Photo Credit**
  Marta Majewska

Well-known food blogger and passionate food stylist Marta Majewska created *Luscious*—a magazine about the art of food—after sharing her ideas online for a few years. The magazine's design and branding focus more on the art of food styling than food itself. Vintage styling, minimalism, simplicity and discreet typography are used in the magazine's layout, allowing the charming photography to be the star.

QUAIL EGGS
WITH SEA
SALT

Ingredients

15 quail eggs
1 tbsp sea salt

Method

Fill a small saucepan with water
and bring to the boil. Add the
quail's eggs using a spoon. Boil for
3 minutes. Remove with a spoon
and cool down under cold running
water. Peel carefully.

Serve with sea salt.

MIn a large skillet, heat olive oil over
medium heat and sauté until the
Brussels sprouts start to soften,
about 4 minutes. Season with salt.

Toast bread on both sides.
Spoon a generous amount of the
Brussels sprouts mixture on each
toast. Sprinkle bruschettas with
Goji berries.

POMEGRATE
APERITIF

Ingredients

750ml cava or champagne
350ml pomegranate juice

Method

Fill 12 flutes with cava or
champagne. Add pomegranate
juice to each flute and serve.

CHIANG MAI

Thailand is a country with a diverse offering where each region has its own unique charm. Chiang Mai, the unofficial capital of Northern Thailand, is best known for its serene temples, hill tribes and bustling markets. Surrounded by mountains and lush countryside, this dynamic and modern city attracts millions of tourists each year.

While the temperatures are dropping below zero in Europe, November through February are the best months to visit Chiang Mai. The rainy season is over and the extremely hot summer months are yet to come.

HOT CINNAMON CHOCOLATE

Ingredients
200g bar dark chocolate
600ml almond milk
100ml whipping s
4 tsp cinnamo

OVEN BAKED SUMMER VEGGIES

Ingredients
200g cherry tomatoes
200g yellow tomatoes
2 zucchinis
2tbs olive oil
Fresh herbs (rosemary, thyme)
Herb salt for seasoning

Method
Preheat the oven to 180°C. Slice the zucchinis lengthwise. Put zucchinis and tomatoes in an angel roasting tray. Scatter rosemary and thyme over the vegetables. Drizzle it all well with olive oil and toss to coat. Add olive oil and seasoning and toss. Bake the vegetables for about 40 minutes. Remove the veggies from the oven and let them rest for a few minutes. Pack into a Tupperware box to transport.

whip the soy cream. In
the chocolate chips,
almond milk,
at, stirring, until
d.
between

Howdy Y'all!

If you're planning on visiting the US
anytime soon and Austin is not on
your to-visit list, you are missing
out! Known for its music scene,
great weather and succulent
barbeque, Austin is the place to
be, especially in spring.
While the rest of the country is
thawing out from the cold winter,
even in early spring Austin's nature
is blooming, parks are getting
crowded and the temperature is
just right!

Ingredients
70g oats
70g cooked quinoa
130ml almond milk
1 tsp maple syrup
1 apple, sliced
Pinch of cinnamon

Method
Preheat the oven to 200°C
degrees. Line a baking tray with
parchment and put apple slices on
it. Bake for 15 minutes.

Add almond milk, maple syrup
and quinoa to a small pot and
bring to boil. Cover, reduce heat
to medium low and simmer for 10-
15min. Add oats and simmer for
another 5 minutes (or until oats are
cooked).

Serve with apples and a pinch of
cinnamon.

David Herbert's Best-Ever Baking Recipes

- **Designer**
  Evi O.

- **Material**
  Uncoated Endpapers,
  Satin Ribbon,
  Head and Tail Band

- **Printing Technology**
  Printed Laminated Cover with
  Matt Lamination

- **Size**
  190mm x 240mm

- **Completion**
  2012

- **Photo Credit**
  Nato Welton

David Herbert is a household name in the United Kingdom and Australia. This book compiles his best baking recipes with the aim of producing a nostalgic yet contemporary looking book.

The design features classic tea towel patterns in vector format and retro pastel colors. Patterned strips are featured down the sides of recipe pages to act as navigational tools, and the rest of the recipe layout is similarly functional. Nostalgic and sweet photography complements the art direction. A slice of chocolate cake is featured on the cover along with embossed typography. The spine highlights three recipes, enticing shoppers to pick the book up when only the spine is visible.

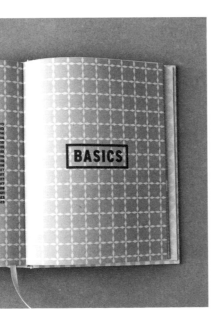

TIPS ON SUGAR

It is essential to add some type of sweetener to most baked goods, to add flavour, tenderness and a bit of 'browning'. This usually comes in the form of sugar, but may also come from honey, golden syrup, maple syrup, treacle or molasses.

Working top to bottom from the image at left, the main varieties are outlined below.

Muscovado sugar is a very dark brown sugar that is used mostly in fruit cakes or where you want biscuits to be soft and chewy. It has a good caramel flavour and a high proportion of molasses. As with all brown sugars, once opened it should be stored in an airtight jar or container. If the sugar dries out, add an apple quarter or slice of bread to the jar for a few days to help it to soften.

Demerara or raw sugar is firm sugar with large crystals. It is more refined than muscovado sugar. It is usually used for sprinkling on the top of cakes, pies, biscuits or muffins before baking as it adds a nice crunchiness when cooked.

Brown sugar is a moist, lightly caramel-flavoured sugar that contains less molasses than muscovado or darker sugars. It is available in dark or light varieties. It is mainly used for cakes, biscuits and some muffins. Store as for muscovado sugar.

Caster sugar is the best choice for cake making - its small grains are easy to combine with other ingredients, ensuring that your cake has a good texture. It is also used in meringues as it dissolves and mixes easily with beaten egg whites. To make vanilla sugar, add 1-2 split vanilla beans to a jar of caster sugar and leave for a couple of weeks for the flavour to develop.

Granulated sugar (or simple white sugar) is the most common variety. In Australia it is made from sugarcane (often in Europe and the United States it is made from sugar beet, a root vegetable).

Icing sugar is a very fine powdery sugar used mostly for icings and dusting cakes and biscuits. It is often used in sweet pastries as it helps create a hard crust. It is available in two forms: 'pure icing sugar' and 'icing sugar mixture'. Icing sugar mixture has a little cornflour added which helps to make a soft icing and also prevents lumps. All references to icing sugar in my recipes are for pure icing sugar. Always sift icing sugar before using so it incorporates more easily.

Golden or unrefined caster sugar is an unrefined small-grained sugar that has a lovely golden colour and a light caramel flavour. It can be used in place of caster sugar - just remember that it will add a slight golden colour so don't use it if you are making white meringues.

Season is a book about celebrating the different times of the year through baking, drawing on the notion that the taste, smell, colors and flavors of food are much more delectable when the food is bought seasonally.

After defining the main theme—baking with fresh ingredients that can only be found at certain times of the year—a visual language was established. The book is divided into four chapters according to the four seasons, and each chapter is defined by the color of the background pictures, from light (summer) to dark (winter). The design and photographs focus on the main character: the ingredients. Minimal props and text are used in the design to allow the food to speak for itself—after all, no words can describe the smell of a cake that's fresh out of the oven.

Season

- **Designer**
  Daniel Farò

- **Material**
  Paper, Cardboard,
  Transparent Vellum

- **Size**
  195mm x 250mm

- **Completion**
  2014

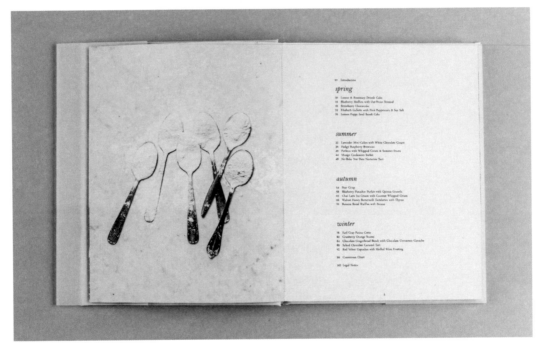

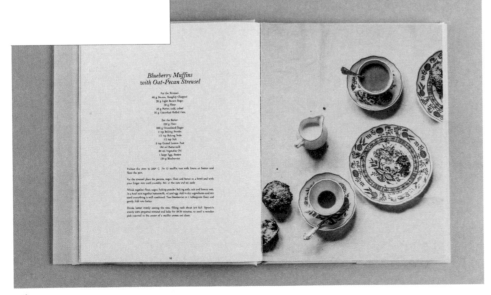

Pavlova with Whipped Cream
& Summer Fruits

4 Egg Whites
200 g Icing Sugar, Sifted
2 tbsp Corn Starch
1/2 tbsp Cocoa Powder
1 tsp Vinegar
400 ml Heavy Cream
Fresh Strawberries
1 tbsp Sugar
Fresh Blueberries
Fresh Raspberries

Preheat the oven to 150° C. Line a cookie tray with parchment paper and set aside.

Put the egg whites in a clean and dry bowl. Using the electric mixer beat the egg whites until soft peaks form. With the mixer still going, slowly add the sugar and beat until the mixture becomes glossy.

Add the corn starch, cocoa powder and vinegar and gently incorporate with a spatula. Spoon the mixture onto the tray and mould it into the shape you desire.

Bake for about 80-90 minutes without opening the oven.

Beat the whipped cream until stiff peaks form. Cut the strawberries and toss them in sugar. Spoon the cream onto the cooled pavlova and top with the fresh fruit.

An Avalanche of Taste

- **Designer**
  Luca di Filippo

- **Material**
  Jacket: Fedrigoni Imitlin Neve;
  Text: 170gsm Matt Paper

- **Printing Technology**
  Silver Foil Printing,
  UV Varnishing

- **Size**
  250mm x 310mm

- **Completion**
  2014

- **Photo Credit**
  Luca di Filippo

- **Publisher**
  Cairo Publishing

This bilingual coffee table cookbook—an ambitious €120,000 project—was born out of the dream of the Chefs and Pastry Cooks Group of Livigno (Italy) who wanted to safeguard and pass on the food and wine traditions of their region.

More than 250 pictures complement 100 traditional recipes and 37 revisited recipes, all compiled by the 38 cooks of the association. The photographic journey balances a classic cookery book approach with innovative storytelling, aiming to merge old tradition and contemporary cuisine into a timeless piece of editorial design. The book's layout elegantly accommodates two languages (Italian and English) without compromising the high-quality visual narrative.

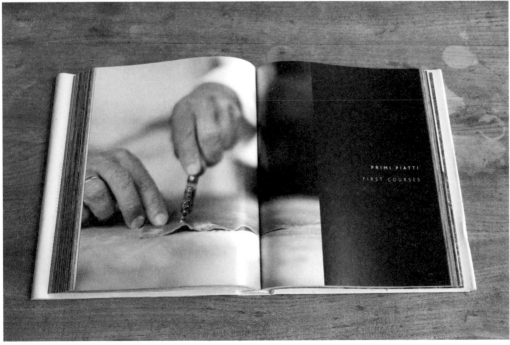

Knife and Fork

- **Design Agency**
  Manuka Studio

- **Material**
  80gsm Paper Munken Print
  White, 300gsm Paper Munken
  Print White

- **Printing Technology**
  Spot Colour Pantone 805C

- **Size**
  210mm x 280mm

- **Completion**
  2015

- **Photo Credit**
  Matys Studio

- **Publisher**
  Civil Society Development
  Foundation (Fundacja
  Rozwoju Społeczeństwa
  Obywatelskiego)

The first issue of the magazine 'Knife and Fork' was published to help small nongovernmental organizations develop their culinary ventures. It contains diverse recipes, everything from a vegan cooperative's favorite dish to a unique syrup made from dandelion flowers.

The publisher's goal was to design a modern, sophisticated, user-friendly culinary magazine. Various design elements are used to this end, including the eponymous 'knife and fork,' which is a stylized design leitmotif throughout the publication. When readers open the front jacket of the magazine, they see a tablecloth inviting them to begin 'the feast.' On the last page, cutlery is arranged as though someone has just finished a good meal (in this case, the magazine).

Two typefaces are used in the publication: modern, friendly Aspira and classical Minion. The layout is complex but flexible, containing various columns and allowing the use of different sized photos, including circular ones. The design is uncluttered and uses lots of white space, allowing the beautiful, uncoated texture of the Munken Print White stock to shine. On the cover, the designers combined a simple color photo with a fresh, Pantone spot color. To emphasize the humanistic, handmade ethos of the recipes, they chose images that show the hands of people standing behind their creations.

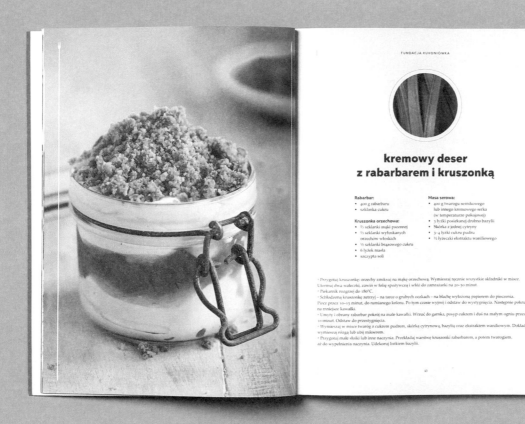

kremowy deser
z rabarbarem i kruszonką

Rabarbar:
- 400 g rabarbaru
- szklanka cukru

Kruszonka orzechowa:
- ½ szklanki mąki pszennej
- ½ szklanki wyłuskanych orzechów włoskich
- ½ szklanki brązowego cukru
- 6 łyżek masła
- szczypta soli

Masa serowa:
- 400 g twarogu sernikowego lub innego kremowego serka (w temperaturze pokojowej)
- 3 łyżki posiekanej drobno bazylii
- Skórka z jednej cytryny
- 3–4 łyżki cukru pudru
- ½ łyżeczki ekstraktu waniliowego

• Przygotuj kruszonkę: orzechy zmiksuj na mąkę orzechową. Wymieszaj ręcznie wszystkie składniki w misce. Uformuj dwa wałeczki, zawiń w folię spożywczą i włóż do zamrażarki na 20–30 minut.
• Piekarnik rozgrzej do 180°C.
• Schłodzoną kruszonkę zetrzyj – na tarce o grubych oczkach – na blachę wyłożoną papierem do pieczenia. Piecz przez 10–15 minut, do rumianego koloru. Po tym czasie wyjmij i odstaw do wystygnięcia. Następnie pokrusz na mniejsze kawałki.
• Umyty i obrany rabarbar pokrój na małe kawałki. Wrzuć do garnka, posyp cukrem i duś na małym ogniu przez 10 minut. Odstaw do przestygnięcia.
• Wymieszaj w misce twaróg z cukrem pudrem, skórką cytrynową, bazylią oraz ekstraktem waniliowym. Dokładnie wymieszaj rózgą lub ubij mikserem.
• Przygotuj małe słoiki lub inne naczynia. Przekładaj warstwę kruszonki rabarbarem, a potem twarogiem, aż do wypełnienia naczynia. Udekoruj listkiem bazylii.

TEKST Jasmine Szymańska •
ZDJĘCIE Kinga Błaszczyk-Wójcicka

smak
kraju, którego
nie ma

manty

Ciasto:
- 2–3 szklanki mąki
- 1 jajko
- 1 szklanka wody
- szczypta soli

Farsz wegetariański:
- 300 g dyni
- 150 g cebuli
- sól, świeżo zmielony pieprz (dużo)

Farsz mięsny:
- 200 g mięsa wołowego bez kości (wg Mahfirat najlepsza jest jednak baranina)
- 180 g dyni
- 100 g cebuli
- sól, świeżo zmielony pieprz

• Dynię i cebulę pokrój w kostkę średniej wielkości. W wersji mięsnej posiekaj drobno wołowinę. Wszystko dopraw solą i dużą ilością pieprzu, żeby manty nabrały ostrości.

• Wsyp do miski 2 szklanki mąki i wbij jajko, dolej wody i dodaj odrobinę soli. Zagnieć wszystkie składniki. Ciasto powinno być sprężyste, nie może kleić się do rąk. Jeśli jest inaczej, dodaj odrobinę mąki i znów zagniataj. Przykryj lnianą ściereczką wyrobione już ciasto i zostaw na kilka minut, żeby odpoczęło.

• Ciasto cienko rozwałkuj i wykrawaj kółka. Możesz też zrobić z ciasta małe kulki i rozwałkować każdą oddzielnie na cienkie, okrągłe placki (ok. 10 cm średnicy). Dużą łyżką nakładaj farsz. Sklejaj brzegi, zawijając w warkoczyk. Uformuj sakiewkę.

• Ułóż gotowe manty na dnie parowaru posmarowanym olejem. Manty mięsne gotuj 25 minut, a wegetariańskie – 15 minut.

• Wyłącz gaz i zostaw przykryty parowar na kolejne 5 minut.

– Po co? – pytam. – Nie wiem – odpowiada ze śmiechem Mahfirat – ale mama tak zawsze robiła. Widać tak trzeba.

35

---

syrop z kwiatów mniszka lekarskiego
Skarby na zdrowie

Syrop z mniszka lekarskiego ma działanie przeciwwirusowe i przeciwzapalne. Zalecany jest przy kaszlu i bólach gardła oraz w leczeniu dolegliwości żołądkowych. Można go kupić albo zrobić samemu.

Na syrop odpowiedni jest tylko mniszek majowy. Kwiaty trzeba zebrać w słoneczny dzień, około południa, po opadnięciu rosy. Inaczej syrop się nie uda.

Żeby zrobić 20 słoików syropu, potrzebujesz 1400 kwiatów mniszka, czyli 54 gramy płatków. Tu przyda się dokładna waga i aptekarska dokładność.

Ostrymi nożyczkami zetnij żółte płatki ze świeżo zerwanych kwiatostanów.

Zalej czterema litrami zimnej wody i gotuj przez godzinę na wolnym ogniu, po czym dobrze odciśnij na sicie lub przez gazę.

Dodaj do wywaru 4 kilogramy cukru i sok z 4 cytryn (150 ml). I znów gotuj na wolnym ogniu przez ok. 120 minut, aż do uzyskania konsystencji płynnego miodu.

Przelej gorący syrop do czystych słoików i szczelnie zakręć. Syrop zachowuje swoje właściwości przez kilka miesięcy od przygotowania.

42   43

Eat Up
Your Life

- **Designer**
  Dmitriy Vepryntsev

- **Material**
  150gsm Coated Paper

- **Printing Technology**
  UV Varnish

- **Size**
  189mm x 246mm

- **Completion**
  2015

'Eat Up Your Life' was made in collaboration with international food company Président. The author, Dmitriy Vepryntsev, compiled his 40 favorite dairy-based recipes incorporating the company's products. This is a book for anyone who likes to eat well, especially when it comes to cheese—the major ingredient in the book—where gourmet experiments have no limits! The food photography and book design share the quality of warmth that a homemade meal brings to a family dinner table.

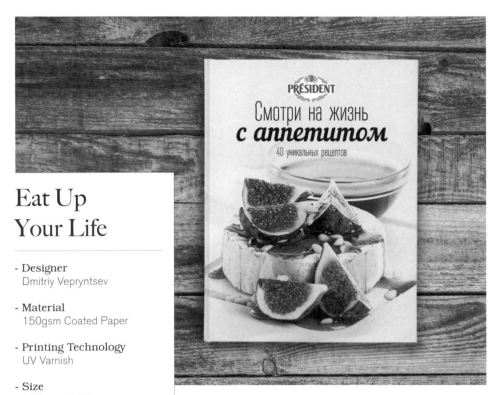

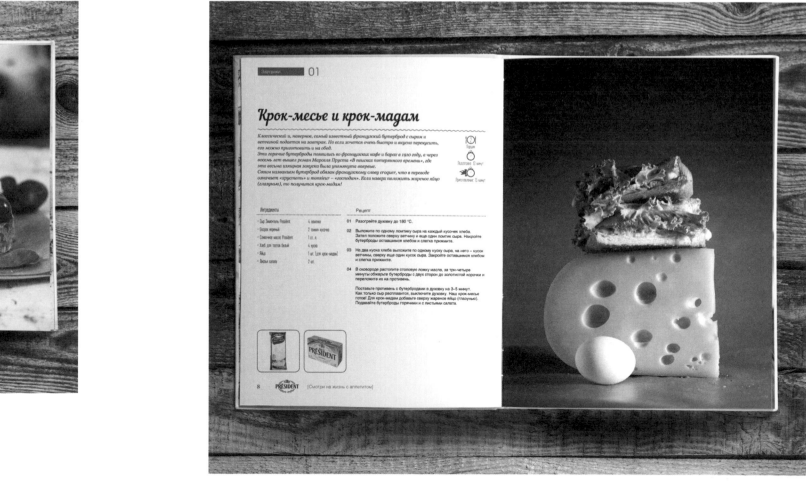

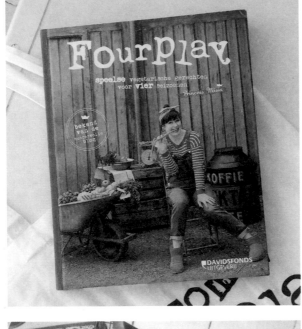

Fourplay

- **Designer**
  Ewelina Bocian

- **Size**
  195mm x 250mm

- **Completion**
  2014

- **Photo Credit**
  Marta Majewska

- **Publisher**
  Davidsfonds

Fourplay: Playful Vegetarian Recipes for Four Seasons presents the work of Belgian food blogger Marta Majewska. It's a book that will appeal as much to cooking enthusiasts as photography lovers.

Recipes in the book are presented in three parts—lead role, supporting role and plot—which gave designer Ewelina Bocian the idea of creating a theatrical mood with the layout. Each recipe's spread is based around a theater poster concept (the book's sexy–clever title also worked well with this idea). As typography plays a significant role in poster design, the recipe titles each have a different composition, balance and color, as if announcing the names of new plays.

Vintage-style photography is used, and each spread's color scheme matches the tones in the photographs. To strengthen the vintage theme, an old-fashioned, typewriter-style font was used throughout the book.

in de OVen geROOSterde radiJzen

± 4 porties

In de hoofdrol

1 bosje radijzen
1 bosje witpuntradijzen

In de bijrol

3 takjes tijm
1,5 eetlepel olijfolie
1 theelepel zeezoutvlokken

Scenario

Verwarm de oven voor op 200°C. Maak de radijzen schoon, verwijder de blaadjes. Leg de radijzen in een ovenschaal. Voeg de olijfolie, de takjes tijm en het zeezout toe. Meng alles. Bak in de oven gedurende 30-40 minuten, tot de radijsjes zacht zijn. Prik er met een vork in om na te gaan of ze gaar zijn. Serveer als hapje of in een salade.

35

COurgette maisBUrgers

± 6 burgers

Scenario

Kook water in een pot en doe de mais erin. Kook 5-8 minuten tot de mais zacht is. Laat afkoelen en haal de maiskorrels van de kolf. Rasp de courgette. Leg ze uitlekken in een zeef of op een zuivere keukenhanddoek en knijp het overtollige vocht eruit. Doe de kikkererwten in een mixer of keukenrobot en pureer. Meng de courgette, de mais, de kikkererwten, de ui en een ei in een kom. Breng op smaak met peper en zout en maak hamburgers van dit mengsel. Strooi de speltbloem op een bord en giet een geklutst ei op een ander bord. Wentel de burgers eerst in de bloem, dan in het ei. Giet een bodempje olijfolie in een pan en verhit. Bak de burgers aan beide zijden goudbruin.

Dien op met een volkorenbroodje, sla, een schijfje avocado en een scheut zelfgemaakte mayonaise.

hoofdrol

1 maïskolf (of 100 g mais uit blik, uitgelekt)
2 courgetten

in de bijrol

100 g kikkererwten
1 middelgrote ui, fijngesneden
2 eieren
50 g speltbloem
olijfolie
peper
zout

50

gele paprikAgazpaCHO

In de hoofdrol

8 gele paprika's

In de bijrol

2 sjalotten
2 teentjes knoflook
500 ml groentebouillon, koud
50 ml olijfolie
3 takjes tijm
& extra om te versieren
peper
zout

Scenario

Verwarm de oven voor op 200°C. Snij de paprika's middendoor en verwijder de pitjes. Leg ze op een met bakpapier beklede bakplaat met de open kant naar onderen. Voeg tijm toe en bak in de oven gedurende 45-60 minuten tot de schil zwart begint te worden. Laat afkoelen en pel de paprika's. Pel de sjalotten en de teentjes knoflook. Doe de sjalotten, knoflook, groentebouillon, olijfolie en

boerenkool-chips

4 porties

In de hoofdrol

3 handen vol boerenkool

In de bijrol

2 eetlepels olijfolie
zeezoutvlokken

Scenario

Verwarm de oven voor op 170°C. Bekleed twee bakplaten met bakpapier. Haal de blaadjes van de boerenkool, spoel ze en dep ze zachtjes droog. Doe de blaadjes in een grote kom. Besprenkel met de olijfolie en masseer elk blaadje met de hand in de olie. Haal je blaadjes er een voor een uit en verdeel ze over de bakplaat zodat elk blaadje dicht bij elkaar. Leg ze niet te over de bakplaat is met de blaadjes niet te dicht bij elkaar. Leg de gedurende ongeveer 12 minuten. Verdeel verschillen, dus kijk er op zodat ze kunnen worden, maar voor ze krokant worden, dus kijk er regelmatig naar. Haal ze uit de oven worden (dan worden ze bitter). Eens worden, breng je ze op smaak met...

158

roDe bieten piZZa

3 pizza's

In de hoofdrol

600 g rode bieten, geschild en gekookt

In de bijrol

30 g gist
200 ml lauw water
500 g speltbloem
600 g manouri (schapenkaas)
50 g noten, naar keuze
2 eetlepels olijfol...

Verwarm de oven voor 180°C. Meng de gist met lauwe water en roer. het werkblad een berg bloem met in het midd kuiltje. Voeg vervolge gistmengsel en de olij en kneed alles tot een deeg ontstaat. Doe het een kom en bedek de me vochtige doek. Zet het d een warme plaats gedure 30 minuten. Pureer de bieten met een staafmixer of in de keukenrobot. Doe het deeg op een met bloem bestrooi werkblad en kneed geduren 2 minuten. Verdeel het dee drie gelijke stukken. Rol e stuk uit met een deegrolle Verdeel de gepureerde rode over de pizza's. Verkruimel manouri erover en bestrooi met de noten. Bak in de oven gedurende 20 minuten of tot de pizza klaar is.

175

Quinoa-frambozenmuFFins

± 10 muffins

In de bijrol

250 g speltbloem
1 eetlepel bakpoeder
0,5 theelepel bicarbonaat
25 ml kokosolie
120 ml ahornsiroop
1 ei
175 ml amandelmelk
50 g tricolore quinoa, klaargemaakt volgens de instructies

In de hoofdrol

125 g frambozen

Scenario

Verwarm de oven voor op 180°C. Meng speltbloem, bakpoeder en bicarbonaat. Smelt de kokosolie op lage temperatuur. Meng de kokosolie met de ahornsiroop, het ei en de amandelmelk. Voeg beide mengsels samen en meng kort (anders krijg je taaie muffins). Voeg de frambozen en de quinoa toe en roer zachtjes. Neem een muffinblik en vul het met het toe. Bak de muffins goudb...

Ice Kitchen—
50 Lolly
Recipes

- **Designer**
  Peter Roden

- **Printing Technology**
  Spot Varnish, Spot Color

- **Size**
  170mm x 220mm

- **Completion**
  2014

- **Photo Credit**
  Adam Slama, Peter Roden

This book was designed to convey a contemporary approach to ice lollies, highlighting the innovative flavors and preparation methods of the New York–based Ice Kitchen business. The clever typeface for the book was designed to reflect melting ice, as well as the lollies' hand-crafted and non-uniform production methods.

Photography of the lollies was done in a clean and simple style, keeping things neutral but contemporary. Images are balanced with bars of natural color, using the rule of thirds to divide each page. Colors were selected to complement different lollies and given a textured treatment that alludes to hand printing, in line with the artisan Ice Kitchen business.

Illustrations feature prominently in the book, their handmade qualities both complementing and contradicting the uniformity of the photography. This artisan treatment further references the business that the book is based on. The combination of the illustration

and photography makes the lollies look so appetizing that you want to pick them up off the page.

For the purpose of international publication, the book's designer, Peter Roden, created many additional glyphs to suit different languages.

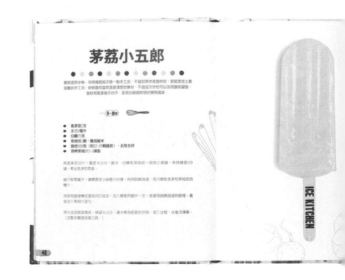

TWIST FRANCÉS

• • • • • • • • • • • • • • • • •

El matrimonio entre la vainilla francesa y las frambuesas funciona a la perfección, y explica por qué este polo es tan popular en nuestro carrito. El toque de vodka impide que las frambuesas se congelen por completo.

8–10

Para las frambuesas:
- 500 g de frambuesas (frescas o congeladas)
- 100 g de azúcar granulado
- 2 cucharadas de vodka (opcional)

Para la vainilla francesa:
- 400 ml de leche entera
- 200 ml de crema de leche espesa
- una pizca de sal
- 1 vaina de vainilla
- 4 yemas de huevo
- 120 g de azúcar granulado

Ponga las frambuesas en un cuenco y añada el azúcar y el vodka. Resérvelas durante un mínimo de 1 hora o toda la noche para que liberen sus zumos.

Para preparar la vainilla francesa, ponga la leche, la crema y la sal en un cazo a fuego lento. Corte la vaina de vainilla a lo largo y raspe las semillas sobre el cazo; añada también la vaina. Bata las yemas y el azúcar en un cuenco refractario. Cuando la leche empiece a hervir, retírela del fuego y añada unas cucharadas a la mezcla de huevo. Bata bien e incorpore de nuevo al cazo. Caliente a fuego medio-bajo, sin dejar de remover, hasta que espese lo suficiente para cubrir el dorso de una cuchara de madera. No deje que hierva. Pase la mezcla por un tamiz fino y deje enfriar. A continuación, refrigere un mínimo de 2 horas.

Triture ligeramente las frambuesas, pero conserve algunas casi enteras. Rellene los moldes de los polos con capas alternas de frambuesa y vainilla. Deje 5 mm libres en la parte superior para permitir que la mezcla se expanda durante la congelación. Mueva un poco las capas con un palo. Introduzca los palos y congele. En la página 22 se explica el procedimiento completo.

92

EGYPTIAN HIBISCUS & PEACH

• • • • • • • • • • • • • • • •

The ancient Egyptian hibiscus drink called 'karkadé' inspired this sweet and tart, ruby-coloured lolly. It is very popular in Egypt where our family came from and in the Sudan where my grandparents and Cosmo's great grandparents once lived. You can find dried hibiscus in most Middle Eastern shops.

8–10

- 40g dried hibiscus, briefly rinsed in cold water
- 850ml water
- 125g plus 2 tablespoons granulated sugar
- 2 peaches, pitted and cut into slim wedges

Put the hibiscus and water in a medium saucepan, bring to the boil and simmer for 5 minutes. Remove the pan from the heat and stir in the 125g sugar. Allow the mixture to steep for a few hours.

Strain the mixture through a fine sieve, pressing on the hibiscus with the back of a spoon to extract the liquid, or squeeze it with your hands. Put the peaches in a small bowl, sprinkle with the 2 tablespoons of sugar and allow them to macerate for 30 minutes. Put a few macerated peach slices and their juices into each ice-lolly mould, then pour the hibiscus mixture in, leaving 5mm at the top to allow the mixture to expand when it freezes. Insert the lolly sticks and freeze. (See page 22 for the complete procedure.)

Variations:
Mix 1 teaspoon orange blossom or rose water, or 1 teaspoon freshly grated ginger into the hibiscus water after you take it off the heat, or mix it into the peaches.

77

BURGUNDY BERRY

• • • • • • • • • • • • • • • •

This mix of berries and wine is great to serve after dinner or at a garden party. Careful not to let your head spin, as too much alcohol will result in a slushy lolly. Pour a little cream at the bottom of each mould for something extra sublime.

8–10

- 250g fresh berries, e.g. raspberries, blackberries, blueberries, plus 170g blackberries
- 140g granulated sugar
- 2 teaspoons freshly squeezed lemon juice
- 125ml Burgundy (or red wine of your choice)
- 125ml water
- 100ml double cream (optional)

Put the 250g fresh berries in a bowl, stir in 80g of the sugar, and the lemon juice and set aside to macerate for at least 1 hour until the juices are released.

Meanwhile, put the wine, water, the 170g blackberries and remaining sugar in a food processor and gently blend. Pour the mixture through a fine sieve over them, stirring with a spoon and pressing down to extract all the juices.

If using the cream, drizzle a teaspoon into each ice-lolly mould, then loosely press the macerated berries into each mould and pour the wine mixture over them, leaving 5mm at the top to allow the mixture to expand when it freezes. Insert the lolly sticks and freeze. (See page 22 for the complete procedure.)

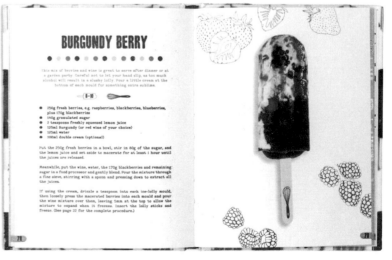

78

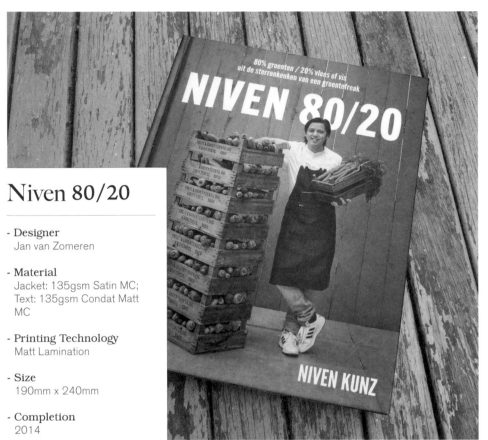

Niven 80/20

- **Designer**
  Jan van Zomeren

- **Material**
  Jacket: 135gsm Satin MC;
  Text: 135gsm Condat Matt
  MC

- **Printing Technology**
  Matt Lamination

- **Size**
  190mm x 240mm

- **Completion**
  2014

- **Photo Credit**
  Jeroen van der Spek,
  Daniel Maissan

This book by chef Niven Kunz represents an 80/20 food philosophy, whereby vegetables and fruit ideally make up 80 percent of a meal, meat or fish the other 20 percent. For Kunz, this 80/20 split is clear and logical and can also be applied in other ways: buying 80/20 organic/nonorganic food, or 80/20 local/imported produce.

In 70 recipes, Kunz shows that cooking with vegetables as the starring instead of supporting role is anything but boring. The recipes are brought to life by superb photography and peppered with useful tips, including suggestions for matching wines.

Since the design brief was to present Kunz as a young, enthusiastic cook, the book had to be accessible and not too 'cheffy' or high-end. To this end, the typeface used is Archer, a friendly and legible font, and the layout is clean and simple.

ABRIKOOS, YOGHURT EN GROVE MOSTERD

ROMANESCO EN FRAMBOOS ON A STICK

RODE BIET EN VIOLETTE MOSTERD

GROENTEN VAN DE GRILL

*Dit gerecht laat zien dat grillen niet alleen
een feestje voor carnivoren is.*

INGREDIËNTEN

- 1 aubergine, geschild
- 1 rode paprika
- 1 knolraap, geschild
- 1 gele courgette, geschild
- 1 meiknol, geschild
- 4 groene asperges, geschild
- 1 winterpeen, geschild
- 8 takjes kervel
- 8 takjes platte peterselie
- paars viooltjes
- mosterd cress
- olijfolie
- Maldon zeezout
- zout en peper, naar smaak

NODIG

- Monolith grill

BEREIDING

Groenten
Snij alle groenten in rechte stukken. Blancheer in gezouten
water. Dompel in ijswater en hou apart. Verwijder de zaad-
lijsten van de paprika.

Roosteren
Besprenkel de groenten met olijfolie, Maldon zeezout, zout
en peper en rooster ze op de grill.

PRESENTATIE

Schik alle groenten op een bord. Besprenkel met olijfolie,
Maldon zeezout en wat peper. Garneer met vioolblaadjes,
kervel, peterselie en mosterd cress.

WIJNTIP

Wit? Een rijke chardonnay. Rood? Een licht gekoelde Proven-
çaalse wijn. Domaine de Triennes uit de Var heeft een goede
blend van cabernet en syrah.

The designers of this book by renowned chef Yotam Ottolenghi wanted to create something that had a visual link to his earlier book, *Plenty*, but with its own strength and character. They came up with an iconic cover that is recognizable, simple, and powerful, and used the same style to create illustrations for each of the chapter openers. Creating a moment of calm between each chapter, these illustrations help to slow the pace of the book.

The illustrations are deliberately intended to contrast with the photographic style used in the book, so as not to compete with the richness of the shots. Vibrant and highly colorful photographs showcase the wide range of ingredients used by Ottolenghi. *Plenty More*'s text design echoes the earlier book, but still maintains its own identity and is intended to feel like a modern, classic book.

Plenty More

- **Design Agency**
  Here Design

- **Material**
  Gloss Art Paper

- **Printing Technology**
  Matt Lamination, Spot UV

- **Size**
  203mm x 277mm

- **Completion**
  2014

- **Photo Credit**
  Here Design

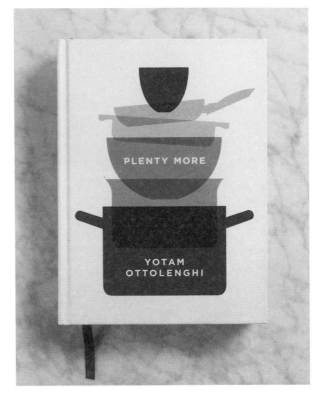

The Spice
Merchant

- Designer
Melissa Hawkett

- Material
148gsm Paper Stock

- Size
200mm x 250mm

- Completion
2013

- Photo Credit
Melissa Hawkett

- Publisher
Blurb

The Spice Merchant is a visually focused cookbook that educates readers about history, culture and flavor through recipes that follow ancient trade routes. It includes spice-based recipes from around the world rather than focusing on one specific cuisine.

This allowed the authors to explore how travel and trade have influenced iconic dishes from different cultures; this research also contributed to the book's design concept. Modern full-bleed food photography is paired with more rustic, organic-style recipes to show the food clearly but give the book an atmosphere of age and authenticity. The typography, textures and illustrative elements are handcrafted, aged and imperfect, referencing old shipping containers and boxes.

The project was a collaboration between designer Melissa Hawkett and chef Hansraj Gengaradoo. They worked closely throughout the production process, planning recipes, cooking and styling the food.

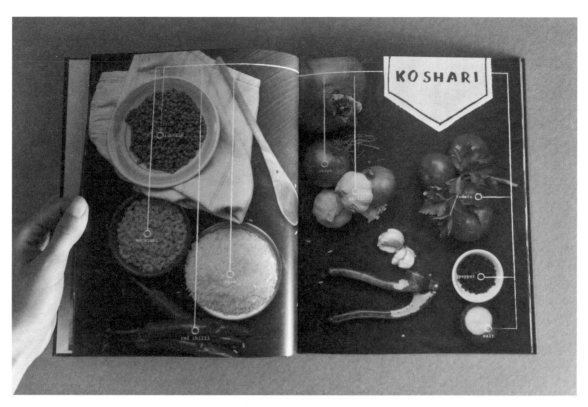

White—The Cookbook

- **Designer**
  Haley Renken

- **Size**
  215mm x 215mm

- **Completion**
  2015

- **Photo Credit**
  Haley Renken

- **Publisher**
  Lulu

This project came about when author Haley Renken wanted to explore the color white's role in culinary experiences. The cookbook contains 17 recipes, including appetizers, mains, sides, desserts, and drinks, that are created using only white ingredients (all are also posted on myrecipes.com). How appetizing is food without hints of color? Can our sensory capabilities still perceive food to be tasty without necessarily being pleasing to the eye? Does white food relate to perceptions of sterility? All answers can be found in this book.

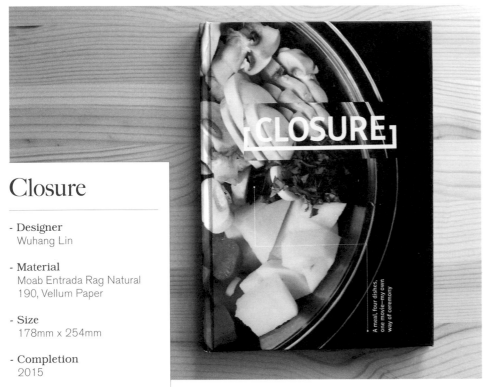

Closure

- **Designer**
  Wuhang Lin

- **Material**
  Moab Entrada Rag Natural
  190, Vellum Paper

- **Size**
  178mm x 254mm

- **Completion**
  2015

- **Photo Credit**
  Wuhang Lin

Closure records the preparation of a meal that designer Wuhang Lin hosted in response to a brief asking her to record a certain event or story. There are two story lines in the book, the main one being the actual process of preparing the meal. The second one comprises quotes from the movie *The Disappearance of Eleanor Rigby*. Two different typefaces are used to separate the main story line from the side subjects.

These narratives create a visual language that combines the composure Lin tries to maintain with the emotions she simultaneously tries to restrain throughout the cooking process. She uses a bold, hand-drawn font to represent the aggressive emotion she feels.

TO MY FRIENDS,
WHO STAY WITH
ME, WHENEVER I'M
BEING A TOXIC
MUSHROOM OR
A SHARP ONION.

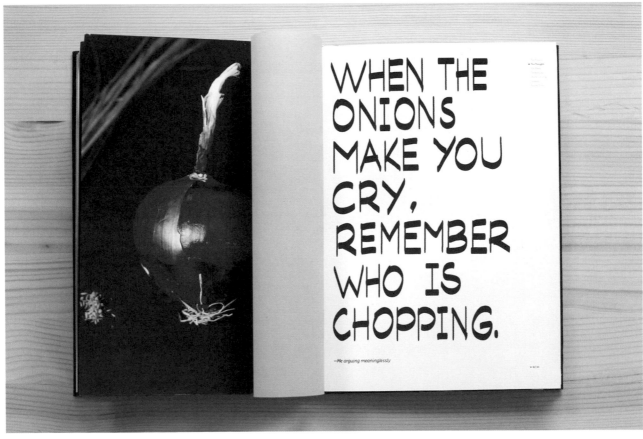

WHEN THE
ONIONS
MAKE YOU
CRY,
REMEMBER
WHO IS
CHOPPING.

—Me arguing meaninglessly

> "I was going to say something really good. And it would have solved all our problems and made everything all better. I just forgot what it was."
>
> —Conor, The Disappearance of Eleanor Rigby: Her

TIPS:

A good dark chocolate combines rich bitterness with a subtle taste of sour and sweet. It is like memory. Memory has never come along purely sad or happy. They usually leave you either a sweet sadness, or a sad sweetness.

No matter how sad or confused I was, I always remember his goodness. I regret, but I don't hate. Him, in opposite, he could not forgive. He acts like he was the only one got hurt, and if I was hurt, I deserved it. How bitterness it is...

Sacher Torte is a specific type of dark chocolate cake invented by Austrian Franz Sacher in 1832 for Prince Wenzel von Metternich in Vienna. It is one of the most famous Viennese culinary specialties. The cake consists of a dense chocolate cake meringue based with a thin layer of apricot jam on top, coated in dark chocolate icing on the top and sides. It is traditionally served with unsweetened whipped cream.

In general, there are three different ways to make cakes. The way to make Sacher Torte is a complicating one. Firstly, you need to separate the egg yokes from the egg white carefully. The egg white need to be kept clean and cool. Then, You beat the sugar with the room temperature soft butter until they get creamy. After that, you add the egg yokes one by one, keep beating until the mixture get creamy, again. Now, you will add in the melted dark chocolate that you have prepared previously and well mix them. Well, it is all about well beating, getting creamy. But when you add in the flour and the baking powder, you need to kind of fold them in gently. No more beating, but still need to well mixing. Well, then you start beating again. You will beat the liquid egg white until they get puffy and creamy. Finally, you will gently fold the puffy egg white into the mixture, and that's it—send it to the oven and bake it for about 45 minutes or so.

I could have chosen to make any cakes with a simple easy recipe, but I like making Sacher Torte for people I care. I enjoy all these complicating and tedious steps of beating and folding. I love to release my love into these well beating and gentle folding process. I don't think I've ever failed to make a good Sacher Torte. But I screwed up a relationship. Apparently, making Sacher Torte is way easier than keeping a guy.

We had a lunch together the other day. He still held bitterness toward me and again he blamed me for being mean to him, which resulted in whatever happened afterward. Does one holding such bitterness deserves a good meal that I prepare with love?

NOPE!

I should share my meal, my ceremony with my friends, who love me indeed.

SACHER TORTE · Fifth Dish

The Recipe:
1. eggs
2. butter
3. flour
4. dark chocolates
5. powdered sugar
6. baking powder
7. apricot jam

How:
It is complicated...

R FELT YOUR

REMEMB WHO IS CHOPPING

—Me arguing meaninglessly

Traveling with Taste

- **Designer**
  Irina Ratsek

- **Material**
  Enamel Paper

- **Printing Technology**
  Glossy Offset Varnish

- **Size**
  220mm x 292mm

- **Completion**
  2014

- **Photo Credit**
  Dmitri Penkov

- **Publisher**
  Mark Media Group Publishing
  House (MMG; Rostov-on-Don,
  Russia)

This original project is a regular annual publication of Russia's Mark Media Group. In this second edition, well-known inhabitants of Rostov-on-Don share recipes of dishes they've tasted while traveling the world. Usually, recipe books only have one or two authors, so these 70 'tasty trips' make for a truly collective mind!

The book is divided into three chapters: Europe, Asia and the New World. Title pages open each section of the book and are followed by author spreads. Fashion shots of contributors are shown on each spread's left-hand side, while the right-hand page is dedicated to their recipes, including food photography executed in the style of the country represented. Similar colors and details merge the left and right pages, making for a very harmonious design.

АННА
ШЕМУРАТОВА,
дизайнер

АНАТОЛИЙ
ШЕМУРАТОВ,
*тренер-консультант,
эксперт в области продаж,
владелец Qoobroom*

Франция, море, вино, устрицы… Предаваться трогательным воспоминаниям, строить планы на будущее, наслаждаться свежим морским ветром и криками чаек. Ловить каждое мгновение, ощущая прикосновения кончиков пальцев любимого человека. Нежное мясо устриц, хрустящий хлеб и бокал холодного белого вина. Черно-белые картинки шедевров Феллини. Обрамлена бархатной французской речью. Сердце замирает, пропуская удар. Все вокруг – стоп-кадр прекрасного кино о любви.

Запеченные устрицы

устрицы Фин де Клер – *2 шт.* | шпинат свежий – *30 г* | сыр пармезан – *10 г*
СОУС: сливки – *60 г* | лук-шалот – *10 г* | вино белое – *20 г* | масло оливковое – *10 г*

Приготовьте соус: нарежьте лук-шалот мелкими кубиками, обжарьте на оливковом масле. Когда лук станет прозрачным, залейте в него вино и тушите, чтобы выпарить алкоголь. Когда вино прокипит как следует, залейте сливки и варите до легкого загустения. Откройте устрицы, выньте мясо, промойте от осколков раковины, положите в готовый соус, еще раз доведите до кипения. В глубокую посуду выложите шпинат, сверху положите припущенную устрицу, полейте соусом и сверху засыпьте тертым пармезаном. Запеките в духовке до образования золотистой корочки.

Забудьте стереотип про зимних и летних УСТРИЦ. Эти деликатесы можно есть круглый год!

МАГА УМХАЕВ,
блогер

Путешествуя однажды по Италии, я остановился в средневековой деревне под Пармой, Сальсомаджоре, в Antico Borgo Castello di Tabiano – это настоящий замок из холмы, вид с которого вскружит голову даже заядлым снобам. При нем уже многие годы существует семейный ресторанчик, в котором из местных продуктов готовят заботливые супруги. Именно там я попробовал свой самый вкусный флорентийский стейк весом в 1500 грамм. Готовили bistecca fiorentina из лучшего мяса на открытом огне, используя оливковые дрова (они не дают дымную, копченую ноту стейку), и до степени прожарки al sangue – красное, сочное, горячее.

Флорентийский стейк

уксус бальзамический – *1 чашка* | масло оливковое – *1 чашка* | розмарин – *¼ чашки* |
стейк портерхаус толщиной 4 см – *1,5 кг* | соль – *2 ч. л.* | перец молотый – *2 ч. л.*

Розмарин мелко нарежьте, смешайте с бальзамическим уксусом и половиной чашки оливкового масла. Влейте смесь в герметичный пакет и положите туда стейк. Запечатайте пакет и уберите в холодильник на ночь, переворачивая мешок несколько раз вечером и утром, перед тем как достать.
Стейк достаньте из холодильника и доведите до комнатной температуры. Духовку разогрейте до 220 °C. Разогрейте сковороду-гриль. Извлеките стейк из маринада, приправьте солью и перцем. Натрите двумя ложками оливкового масла. Обжарьте стейк на умеренном огне по 5 минут с каждой стороны. Переложите на противень и запекайте до температуры в центре куска 52 °C, что примерно эквивалентно 30 минутам. Стейк извлеките из духовки и выложите на разделочную доску. Дайте «отдохнуть» 10 минут.

ЕЛЕНА
КРАСНОЖОН,
директор магазина
Paul&Shark

ЮЛИЯ БУТКО

Мы с уверенностью можем назвать Италию одной из своих любимых стран. Она пленяет неповторимым колоритом, богатой историей и культурой и, конечно, великолепной кухней. Определяющим фактором в выборе пищи для нас выступает не насыщение, а подлинное удовольствие. Впервые попробовав это блюдо, мы с дочерью влюбились в него навсегда, ведь оно как нельзя лучше воплощает в себе все то, что мы ценим в еде, – свежесть, легкость, пользу вкупе с утонченным вкусом.

Гребешок нарежьте мелкими кубиками, заправьте оливковым маслом, лимонным соком и добавьте трюфельную пасту. Приготовьте гарнир для первого тартара: огурец и яблоко очистите от кожи и семян и нарежьте мелкими кубиками, заправьте оливковым маслом и семенами кунжута. Лосось нарежьте мелкими кубиками, добавьте таким же образом нарезанную клубнику с сыром дорблю, заправьте оливковым маслом и лимонным соком. Приготовьте гарнир для этого тартара: помидоры очистите от кожи и семян, нарежьте мелкими кубиками, добавьте рубленый лук, заправьте маслом.
Тунец и мяту нарежьте мелкими кубиками, заправьте кунжутным маслом и лимонным соком. Авокадо посолите, добавьте оливковое масло.
На порционную тарелку с помощью формочек выложите первый гарнир, а поверх – тартар из гребешка. Рядом – второй гарнир, поверх которого – тартар из лосося. Рядом выложите авокадо с маслом и тартар из тунца. Украсьте зеленью.

Трио тартар

гребешок – 100 г | лосось – 100 г | клубника – 30 г | сыр дорблю – 10 г |
паста трюфельная – 10 г | масло оливковое – 2 г | яблоки – 50 г |
тунец консервированный в собственном соку – 100 г | мята – 2 г |
масло кунжутное – 5 г | огурцы – 20 г | семечки кунжутные – 5 г | помидоры – 50 г |
базилик – 2 г | лук красный – 10 г | авокадо – 100 г | сок лимонный – 5 г |
перец красный стручковый – 1 г

23

ДМИТРИЙ
ТАТЬЯНЧЕНКО,
директор туристической
компании «Евролюкс»

Я не только путешествую и занимаюсь бизнесом, но и являюсь мастером спорта по спортивному рыболовству. Все началось еще в детстве, когда я ездил на каникулы к бабушке в Таганрог, где и увлекся рыбалкой. В последнее время очень полюбил Норвегию за восхитительную природу, бескрайние водоемы и вкусную рыбу. Попробуйте – вам понравится!

Треска с диким рисом и ростками папоротника

стейк трески – 1 шт. | масло оливковое – 20 г |
рис дикий – 80 г | ростки папоротника – 30 г | масло сливочное – 20 г |
соль – 2 г | перец – 2 г

Ростки папоротника
в этом рецепте
можно заменить
любой любимой вами
зеленью.

Дикий рис отварите в соленой воде до раскрытия зерен (35–40 минут). Затем обжарьте его в смеси оливкового и сливочного масла. Добавьте в рис ростки папоротника, посолите и поперчите по вкусу, выложите на тарелку.
Стейк трески посолите, поперчите и смажьте оливковым маслом со всех сторон. Обжарьте рыбу на сковороде в течение нескольких минут до золотистой корочки. Выложите треску на тарелку рядом с рисом, украсьте цедрой лимона.

21

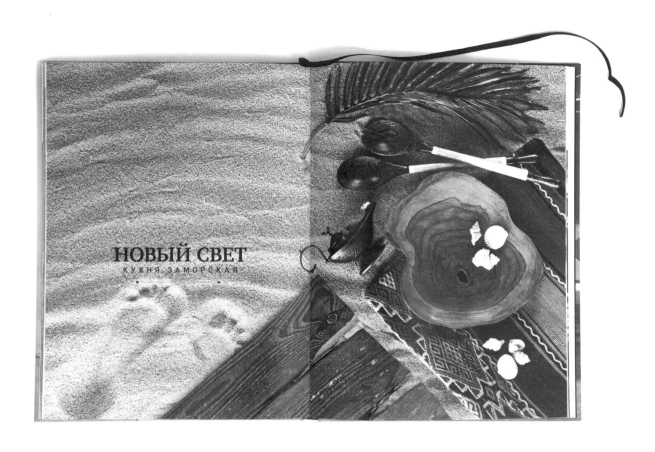

НОВЫЙ СВЕТ
КУХНЯ ЗАМОРСКАЯ

МАКСИМ МИЩЕНКО,
владелец ресто-кафе «Шем-Тов»

ЕВГЕНИЯ МИЩЕНКО,
чемпионка России по фитнесу 2014 года

В прошлом году мы путешествовали с женой по Мексике. Мне было интересно узнать у мексиканцев секреты приготовления пищи – почему они так любят острые вкусы и кладут везде столько зелени. В одной из кафешек мы попробовали необычную для нас вариацию фахитос – с соусом гуакамоле. Теперь этим рецептом смело делимся со всеми, кто не боится острой мексиканской кухни.

Фахитос с соусом гуакамоле

говяжья вырезка – 300 г | перец болгарский красный – 1 шт. |
перец болгарский желтый – 1 шт. | тмин молотый – 10 г | перец чили молотый – 10 г |
паприка – 10 г | масло оливковое – 10 г | петрушка – 10 г | кинза – 10 г |
СОУС ГУАКАМОЛЕ: авокадо – 2 шт. | сок лайма – 1 шт. |
чеснок – 1 зубчик | перец чили – ½ стручка | лук – 1 шт. | помидоры – 2 шт. |
петрушка – 10 г | кинза – 10 г

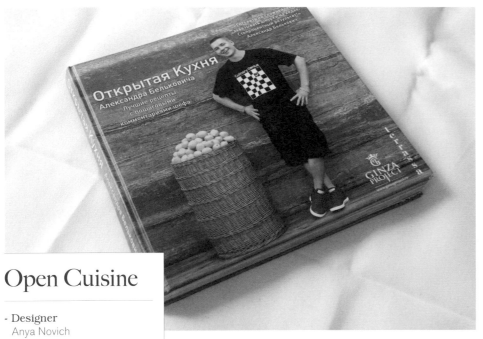

This book was made for Russian restaurant giant, the Ginza Project. Its recipes were created and directed by the restaurant's youngest chef Sasha Belkovich, who also works at Terrassa in the heart of Saint Petersburg. The book's aim was to highlight high-class but warm and hearty food, and Sasha's energetic style of cooking.

Navigation is assisted by the use of colored bars, headings and page numbering in every section of the book. Sections are also preceded by photographic title pages that reflect the content to follow. A square format was chosen to make the book stand out, and beautiful photos of meals are combined with hand-drawn illustrations. As the audience for this book is people who may not be used to cooking at home, every recipe is supplemented with detailed photos of the various cooking processes involved.

Open Cuisine

- **Designer**
  Anya Novich

- **Printing Technology**
  UV Varnishing

- **Size**
  250mm x 250mm

- **Photo Credit**
  Philip Beloborodoff

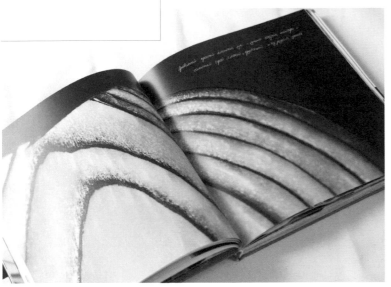

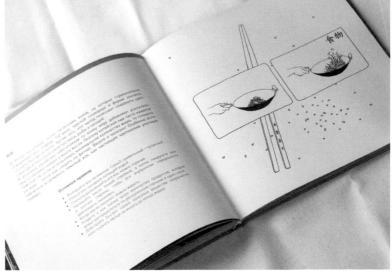

Как разделывать лосося

1. В первую очередь понадобится длинный острый нож. Положить лосося на доску под углом, чтобы было удобнее сделать разрез одним движением.

2. Наискось отрезать голову от туловища с обеих сторон, чтобы захватить плавник, — из нее ещё можно будет сварить суп

3. Сделать продольный разрез вдоль хребта от хвоста к голове Разделить рыбу на две половинки и аккуратно отделить позвоночную кость.

4. Отрезать от получившегося филе крупные кости с краю.

5. Специальными щипцами вынуть мелкие кости. Чтобы обнаружить их, следует провести рукой против направления их роста.

6. Если нужно, снять кожу. Лучше сделать это одним резким движением.

Kid's CooKing

- **Designer**
  Sarah Marie Lau

- **Material**
  90gsm Coated Paper

- **Size**
  170mm x 215mm

- **Completion**
  2012

- **Photo Credit**
  Reiner Schmitz,
  Jason Montague

This is a book for parents who want to cook nutritious food for their kids that's also satisfying for grown-ups. Recipes are grouped into appetizers, snacks, mains, desserts and so on, in line with a classical menu structure, and the book's design reflects this menu theme.

Photographs are an important element of the book layout—the background of the images is simultaneously the background of the typography and other design elements—and images in fresh pastel tones are carefully balanced with the menu themes. The typography and infographics are carefree, playful and a bit rebellious in line with the book's subject.

Mmm!

- **Designer**
  Agnieszka Sowińska

- **Size**
  240mm x 280mm

- **Photo Credit**
  Agnieszka Sowińska

Mmm! is a magazine for lovers of food, with each issue dedicated to just one food product, such as cheese. The designer, Agnieszka Sowińska, eschews a logo for the magazine's cover, and instead creates a typographic composition of *Mmm!* consisting of food and kitchen paraphernalia relating to each issue's food topic. Minimalist design and photography further enhance what are very eye-catching covers, helping the magazine to stand out from its competitors.

The interior pages combine a slab serif font with a handwritten typeface, and different typographic compositions are used throughout the journal. Additionally various useful icons for recipes and other parts of the magazine were developed.

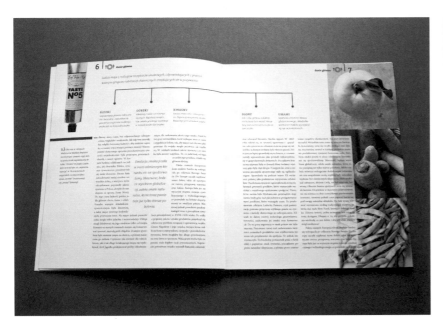

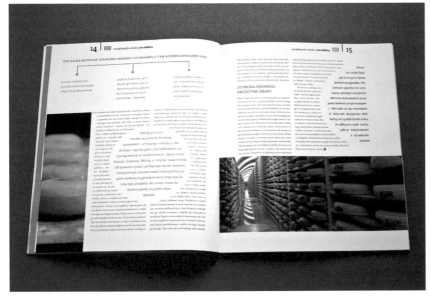

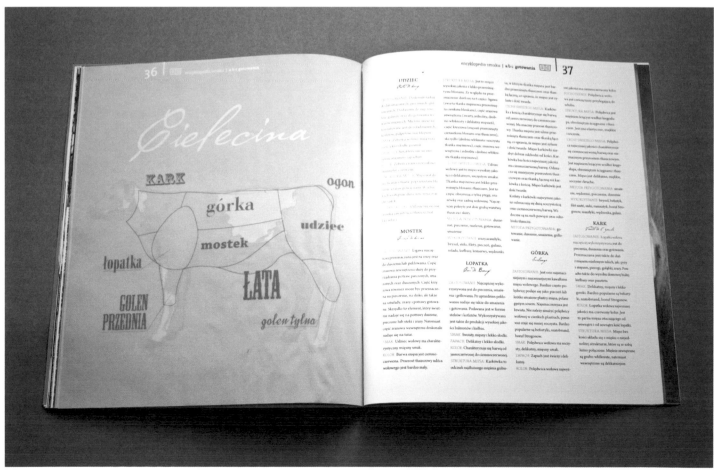

The Ginger & White Cookbook

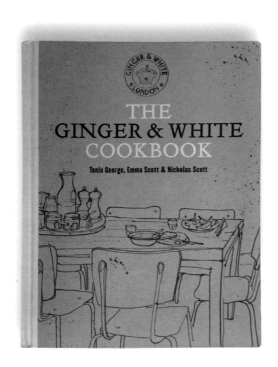

- **Collaborators**
  Tonia George, Emma Scott,
  Nicholas Scott (Authors),
  Juliette Norsworthy (Designer),
  Abigail Read (Illustrator)

- **Size**
  189mm x 246mm

- **Completion**
  2014

- **Photo Credit**
  Jenny Zarins

- **Publisher**
  Mitchell Beazley

London's Ginger & White café is renowned for its wonderful baking, great coffee, and delicious comfort food created from superb artisanal ingredients. Its devoted customers range from toddlers to grannies, all drawn to the family friendly atmosphere and exceptional flavors on offer.

The Ginger & White Cookbook, written by Tonia George, Emma Scott, and Nicholas Scott, is the café's first cookbook. Designer Juliette Norsworthy used a rustic style of illustration alongside a clean and industrial-looking design to reflect the feel, aesthetic, and palette of the café. Illustrator Abigail Read drew the pictures at the café itself to bring touches that define its style onto the pages of the book, such as the industrial enamel lampshades, Kilner jars, and comfy leather sofas.

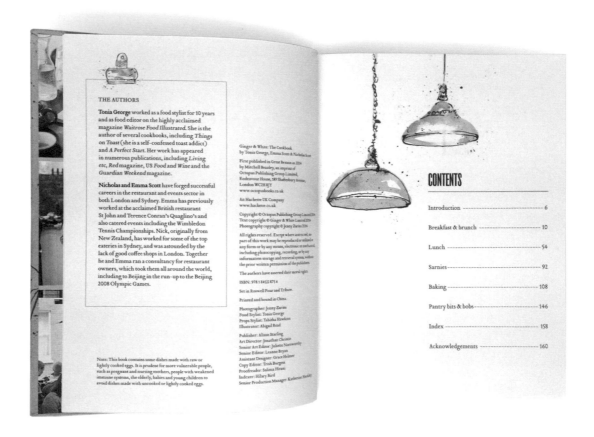

Breakfast & brunch

Hot chocolate
with marshmallows

We use luxurious Montezuma's chocolate, which, when mixed with creamy milk, is pretty much the eighth wonder of the world. Just ask Wendy, our resident hot chocolate connoisseur, who you'll find in our Hampstead branch on any given day. To spice things up a bit, try using chocolate flavoured with mint, chilli or bitter orange.

Put the chocolate and cocoa into an enamel mug. Add the water and stir to make a paste.

Steam the milk, stretching it with your steam wand, or heat on the hob to just below boiling point. Whisk it into the chocolate paste, then float the marshmallows on top and serve straight away.

SERVES 1

2 heaped tbsp grated dark chocolate (at least 70 per cent cocoa solids)

1 heaped tbsp cocoa powder

1 tbsp boiling water

200ml whole milk

2 big marshmallows or a handful of mini ones

Steak with Gentleman's Relish
& tarragon butter

I think we're a bit obsessed with Gentleman's Relish at Ginger & White. It's a salty little number made from anchovies and spices and we offer it on the communal tables alongside brown sauce and ketchup. When we opened in Belsize Park our first chef, Tom, came up with this magnificent butter and now we always keep some in the freezer. It's also great for slathering on roast beef sarnies.

First make the tarragon butter. Blitz the tarragon leaves in a food processor, then add the butter and Gentleman's Relish and blitz again. Roll the butter into a sausage, wrap in clingfilm and store in the refrigerator.

Place a griddle pan over a high heat until really hot. Season the steaks with salt and pepper and brush with oil. Cook for 2 minutes on each side for medium rare, or longer if you prefer your steak medium to well done. Take off the heat and leave to rest for 2 minutes.

Slice and top with a disc or two of the flavoured butter. Serve with mixed salad leaves.

SERVES 2

2 × 250g rump steaks

salt and pepper

olive oil

mixed salad leaves, to serve

For the tarragon butter

2 sprigs of tarragon, leaves only

125g butter, softened

1 tbsp Gentleman's Relish

Baking

Gingerbread grannies

These little gingerbread biscuits sum up our attitude to family: from youngest to oldest, everyone is important. Look out for a gingerbread-lady cutter (with skirt). We like to make our grannies' hair with white icing and sometimes give them a pale blue rinse. We have even been known to add little handbags.

Preheat the oven to 180°C/fan 160°C/gas mark 4. Line 2 baking sheets with nonstick baking paper.

Place the flour, ginger, mixed spice, bicarbonate of soda and salt in a large bowl. Add the butter and pulse in a food processor or rub in with your fingertips until the mixture resembles breadcrumbs.

Put the egg, golden syrup and muscovado sugar into a separate bowl and beat until blended. Pour into the dry ingredients and mix together until a soft dough forms. Wrap in clingfilm and chill for 30 minutes.

Roll out the dough on a lightly floured surface to the thickness of a £1 coin. Using a lady-shaped 10–15cm cutter, stamp out as many grannies as you can. Transfer to the prepared baking sheets and bake for 10–12 minutes, until lightly coloured. Let the biscuits cool on the sheets.

Once cool, decorate the grannies using the icing to draw skirts, hair and glasses, coloured writing icing to mark out eyes and mouths, and silver balls for buttons.

MAKES 15

350g plain flour, plus extra for dusting
1 tbsp ground ginger
1 tbsp ground mixed spice
1 tsp bicarbonate of soda
¼ tsp fine salt
125g cold unsalted butter, cubed
1 free-range egg
4 tbsp golden syrup
150g light muscovado sugar
Lemon Icing (see page 128)
coloured writing icing
edible silver balls

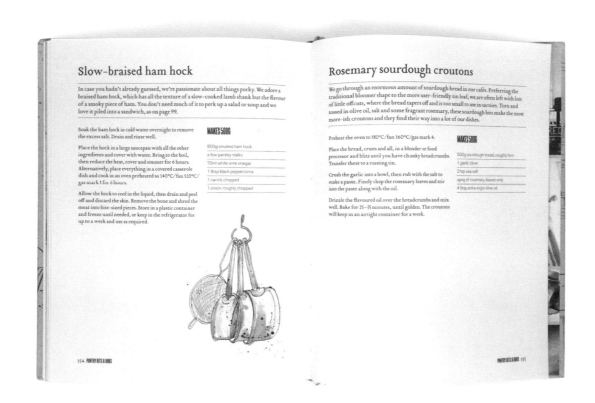

Slow-braised ham hock

In case you hadn't already guessed, we're passionate about all things porky. We adore a braised ham hock, which has all the texture of a slow-cooked lamb shank but the flavour of a smoky piece of ham. You don't need much of it to perk up a salad or soup and we love it piled into a sandwich, as on page 99.

Soak the ham hock in cold water overnight to remove the excess salt. Drain and rinse well.

Place the hock in a large saucepan with all the other ingredients and cover with water. Bring to the boil, then reduce the heat, cover and simmer for 6 hours. Alternatively, place everything in a covered casserole dish and cook in an oven preheated to 140°C/fan 120°C/gas mark 1 for 6 hours.

Allow the hock to cool in the liquid, then drain and peel off and discard the skin. Remove the bone and shred the meat into bite-sized pieces. Store in a plastic container and freeze until needed, or keep in the refrigerator for up to a week and use as required.

MAKES 500G

800g smoked ham hock
a few parsley stalks
70ml white wine vinegar
1 tbsp black peppercorns
1 carrot, chopped
1 onion, roughly chopped

Rosemary sourdough croutons

We go through an enormous amount of sourdough bread in our cafés. Preferring the traditional bloomer shape to the more user-friendly tin loaf, we are often left with lots of little offcuts, where the bread tapers off and is too small to use in sarnies. Torn and tossed in olive oil, salt and some fragrant rosemary, these sourdough bits make the most more-ish croutons and they find their way into a lot of our dishes.

Preheat the oven to 180°C/fan 160°C/gas mark 4.

Place the bread, crusts and all, in a blender or food processor and blitz until you have chunky breadcrumbs. Transfer these to a roasting tin.

Crush the garlic into a bowl, then rub with the salt to make a paste. Finely chop the rosemary leaves and stir into the paste along with the oil.

Drizzle the flavoured oil over the breadcrumbs and mix well. Bake for 25–35 minutes, until golden. The croutons will keep in an airtight container for a week.

MAKES 500G

500g sourdough bread, roughly torn
1 garlic clove
2 tsp sea salt
sprig of rosemary, leaves only
4 tbsp extra virgin olive oil

Children's Birthday Parties

- **Design Agency**
  Cosa Kitchen

- **Printing Technology**
  UV Spot-Varnishing

- **Size**
  200mm x 235mm

- **Completion**
  2015

- **Photo Credit**
  Cosa Kitchen,
  Edition Michael Fischer

- **Publisher**
  Edition Michael Fischer

The biggest day for little ones is their own birthday; it's eagerly awaited like no other event in the year (with the possible exception of Christmas). To make this special occasion perfect for both the excited child and the busy parents, Cosa Kitchen has compiled this beautiful themed parties book, covering everything from first birthdays onwards. Helpful tips to create delicious food and child-friendly decor provide readers with all they need to create a party to remember. Let's celebrate with mischievous monsters, enchanted frog kings, powerful superheroes or wild pirates!

The Mangalitsa

- **Designer**
  David Barath

- **Material**
  130gsm Artic Volume White
  Paper

- **Size**
  185mm x 240mm

- **Completion**
  2012

- **Collaborators**
  Balazs Glodi (Photography),
  Aron Barath (Food Styling),
  Mate Dobesch (Illustrator)

- **Publisher**
  Boook Publishing

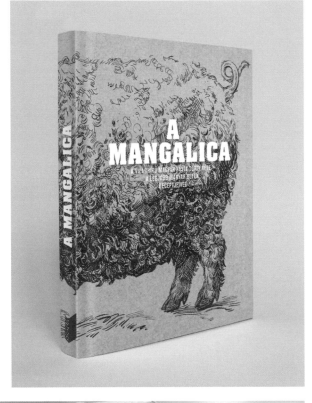

'The Mangalitsa' (*A Mangalica*—the hungarian, original, 1st edition of the title/book) is a Hungarian breed of pork—bigger than regular pigs and with unique curly hair—that was once nearly extinct. Thanks to the gastro revolution and Slow Food movement, however, it's been brought back into the limelight.

The idea for this book was conceived when bistro culture—and, hand in hand with that, pork—became increasingly popular. Indeed, David Barath's design uses fonts and colors, including brown paper on the cover, that echo bistros. The look of the Mangalica was less known at the time of design, so Barath also incorporated a simple drawing of the pig on the cover.

Describing the origins and specifics of the breed, along with the differences between regular pork and Mangalitsa, the book then goes on to list pork recipes provided by some of Hungary's best chefs. Apart from the main font, the internal layout is structured and simple to aid usability.

A MANGALICA HÚSA

01. SZŰZPECSENYE
A rövid karaj gerinccsont alatti színhúsrésze, mely átnyúlik a felsálba. Kifejezetten puha és zsírmentes, ezért süthetjük egészben, szeletben, alacsony hőmérsékleten, vákuumban vagy rántva. Túl hosszú sütés során kiszáradhat, ezért gyakran találják töltve vagy pácolva, esetleg tálalják mártással vagy szósszal.

66. oldal
Mangalicaszűz paprikás burgonyával

80. oldal
Mangalica-szűzpecsenye bébizöldségekkel és pürékkel

104. oldal
Szivarfüstben érlelt szűzpecsenye borjúlábduóval, hagymalekvárral és paradicsombefőttel

170. oldal
Rozmaringos mangalicaszűz sült céklával, zöldborsós árparizottóval

02-03. TARJA
Az állat hátsó, nyaki részén található, meglehetősen zsíros és puha hús. Ritkábban egészben, gyakrabban szeletben sütve, konfitálva, vákuumban, alacsony hőmérsékleten sütve lehet elkészíteni. Általában főételként, steak vagy szelet formában kínáljuk, de hideg sültnek is alkalmas.

40. oldal
Mangalicatarja sült babbal és paradicsommal

64. oldal
Mangalicatarja bükki sajtfondüvel

210. oldal
Mangalicatarja hagymás törtburgonyával és parajjal

04-05. KARAJ
Bordacsonttal és csont nélküli változatban is kapható, szokás rajta hagyni bőr alatti zsírréteget is. Ízletes, kissé száraz hús. Egészben, alacsony hőmérsékleten sütve, vagy vákuumban, illetve rántva lehet elkészíteni

56. oldal
Mangalicakaraj polippal és véres hurkás Anna burgonyával

114. oldal
Mangalicakaraj szarvasgombás hasaalja-szalonnával

138. oldal
Mangalicakaraj citrusos fehérbabmártással és Szent Jakab kagylóval

152. oldal
Mangalicakaraj konfitált mangalicafüllel, rántott vajas zellerpürével, sült sárgarépával

184. oldal
Mangalicakaraj füstölt kenyérszósszal és cukorrépalevelekkel

KÉTSZÍNŰ LEVESDUETT

HOZZÁVALÓK A BURGONYAKRÉMLEVESHEZ (4 FŐRE)
30 dkg lisztes burgonya
80 g vegyes zöldség (salotta- és póréhagyma, zeller, édeskömény)
50 ml fehérbor
500 ml szárnyasalaplé vagy víz
60 ml barnított vaj
1 csapott ek szárított vagy ½ csokor friss turbolya
2 ek laktózmentes tejföl
ízlés szerint fehér balzsamecet, só, fehér bors, szerecsendió, babérlevél

A LECSÓKRÉMLEVESHEZ
20 dkg vöröshagyma
40 dkg paradicsom
20 dkg kaliforniai paprika
60 dkg töltenivaló vagy lecsópaprika
50 g enyhén füstölt mangalica hasaalja
2 ek napraforgóolaj
2 ek főzőtejszín
ízlés szerint só, bors, majoránna

A TÁLALÁSHOZ
20 dkg hízott libamáj
4 szelet három hónapos mangalicasonka

AJÁNLOTT BOR
GÁL TIBOR
VRC (viognier-rajnai rizling cuvée), 2006

A burgonyát és a zöldségeket meghámozzuk, kockákra vágjuk, kevés zsiradékon megfuttatjuk, felöntjük a borral, majd egyharmadára sűrítjük. Felöntjük az alaplével, ízlés szerint fűszerezzük, majd közepes lángon puhára főzzük. Kiemeljük belőle a babérlevelet, krémesre turmixoljuk, majd finom lyukú szűrön átpasszírozzuk, és visszatesszük a tűzre. Hozzáadjuk a tejfölt, ízlés szerint ecetet és fűszereket (ha sűrűnek találjuk, hígítsuk alaplével vagy vízzel). Forraljuk össze, és csak tálalás előtt keverjük bele a barnított vajat (ehhez a vajat addig kell melegíteni, míg karamellszínűre nem barnul).

A paradicsomot leforrázzuk, meghámozzuk, majd gerezdekre vágjuk. A paprikát megmossuk, kocsányát a magléccel és magokkal együtt eltávolítjuk, majd ujjnyi vastag karikákra szeljük. A hagymát meghámozzuk, vékonyszeletekre vágjuk. A szalonnát apró kockákra vágjuk. Az olajhoz adjuk a szalonnát, és mérsékelt tűzön zsírjára pirítjuk. Megfonnyasztjuk rajta a hagymát, rádobjuk a paprikát, átforgatjuk a hagymás-szalonnás zsírral, mérsékelt tűzön tíz percig pároljuk. Hozzáadjuk a paradicsomot, sózzuk, borsozzuk, egy csipet majoránnát is adunk hozzá (fontos, hogy hosszabb lével készüljön, mint a hagyományos lecsó). Turmixoljuk, finom lyukú szűrön átpasszírozzuk, és a tejszínnel sűrítjük.

Tálalásnál a tányérok aljába kb. 1,5 deci lecsókrémlevest teszünk, majd óvatosan a közepébe csorgatunk ennél kevesebb, kb. 1 deci burgonyakrémlevest. A libamájat óvatosan négy szeletre vágjuk, majd serpenyőben közepes lángon zsírjára sütjük. Egy másik serpenyőben a sonkát sütjük ropogósra, a májjal és a sonkával díszítjük a tányért (grissinit is kínálhatunk mellé).

Top book spread

MANGALICACARPACCIO KOVÁSZOSUBORKA-REMULÁDDAL ÉS PAPRIKÁS KALÁCCSAL

HOZZÁVALÓK A CARPACCIÓHOZ (4 FŐRE)
80 dkg mangalicaszűz
(lehetőleg egy darab)
ízlés szerint só, frissen őrölt bors

A REMULÁDHOZ
20 dkg kovászos uborka és annak leve
1 csokor petrezselyem
5 dkg kapribogyó
2 fürjtojás
2 dl extra szűz olívaolaj
ízlés szerint só, frissen őrölt bors

A PAPRIKÁS KALÁCSHOZ
10 dkg barna cukor
10 dkg őrölt fűszerpaprika
2,5 dl tej
40 dkg liszt
2 ek mangalicazsír
2,5 dkg élesztő
2 ek tejföl

AJÁNLOTT BOR
GÁL PINCÉSZET
Pinot Noir Rosé, 2011

A mangalicaszüzet megtisztítjuk a hártyáktól, majd jó erősen besózzuk és beborsozzuk. Felforrósított serpenyőben erős kérget pirítunk rá, majd még melegen a hűtőbe tesszük. Ha kihűlt, akkor átlátszó fóliával betekerjük, hogy szép hengerformát kapjunk, és a fagyasztóba helyezzük.

A remuládhoz a fürjtojás kivételével minden hozzávalót apró kockákra vágunk, összekeverjük, sózzuk és borsozzuk (érdemes egy nappal korábban összeállítani, hogy az ízek összeérjenek). A tojást megfőzzük, és tálalás előtt kettévágjuk.

A kalácshoz a lisztet egy tálba szitáljuk. A tejet szobahőmérsékletre melegítjük, belemorzsoljuk az élesztőt, majd hagyjuk egy kicsit kelni. Ha az élesztő már kifejtette hatását, a tejet a liszthez keverjük, hozzáadjuk a tejfölt és a zsírt is. Langyos helyen kb. 15-20 percig kelesztjük, majd ujjnyi vastagra nyújtjuk a tésztát. A fűszerpaprikát elkeverjük a cukorral, és a tésztára szórjuk, majd feltekerjük, zsírpapírral bélelt sütőre tesszük, és 180 fokra előmelegített sütőbe tesszük. 20-25 percig sütjük, amíg a teteje meg nem pirul, majd kissé hagyjuk kihűlni, és csak ezután szeleteljük.

A szüzet hajszálvékonyra szeletelve a mártással, a fürjtojással és a kaláccsal együtt tálaljuk.

Bottom left book spread

LŐRINCZ GYÖRGY

BABEL

A kezdetektől itt bábáskodott a fine dining egyik legfontosabb hazai szentélye: a Babel létrehozásánál, annak újraynyitásával pedig kulcspozícióban, executive chefként irányítja azt. Hitvallása a vendég – ilyen egyszerűen. Ami azt jelenti, hogy számára a vendégélmény komplexitása a legfontosabb, ízek, hangulatok és látvány olyan együttese, melyet a lehető legjobban kell megfogalmazni annak érdekében, hogy a vendég elégedett legyen.

„Leginkább a tradicionális konyhát kedvelem, így főleg klasszikus és maszkulin alapanyagokat használok. Szeretem az efféléken vagy műfajain túlmutató házírbre szerinteit ételeket, alapanyagokat újra elővenni, és középpontba helyezni – akár eredeti formájukban, akár mai interpretációban. Mindkét esetben elég egy kedves élmény, egy gyerekkori íz, vagy illat felidézése, és máris inspiálnak az ahhoz kapcsolódó pozitív emlékek és hangulatok. Sajátos ember volt rám nagy hatással, ezek körül a nagymamán – neki köszönhetem az alapokat, a sok régi ízt és ízlárom. A magyar konyhában egyébként is ott a sok íze, a fűszerságot, a komplexitást kedvelem. A magyar és a francia konyhát párhuzamosan tartom, főleg maszkulin mivoltuk miatt mindkettőben hangsúlyos és testes ízek, alapanyagok dominálnak, amikor jó arányrendszerrel magasra lehet emelni. A mangalica jó példa erre, hiszen fantasztikus az illaga, mindenféllett nincs meg benne a rossz érzelemben vett sertésíz. Azt gondolom, hogy a világ elindul lassan újra feltfedezni ez elfeledett értékeit, kiaknázni közvetlen könyvezen lehetőségeit. A mangalica renaissa szépen rímel erre a folyamatra, és ez ennek örülök, hiszen a mangalica jó, és a miénk."*

Bottom right book page

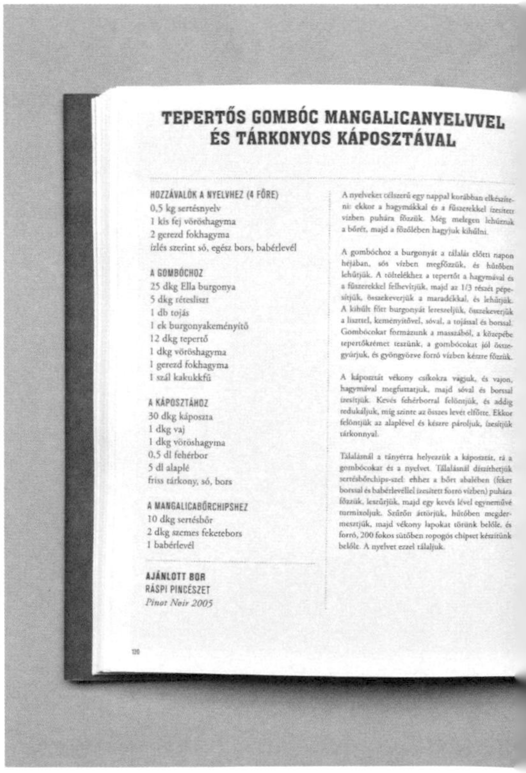

TEPERTŐS GOMBÓC MANGALICANYELVVEL ÉS TÁRKONYOS KÁPOSZTÁVAL

HOZZÁVALÓK A NYELVHEZ (4 FŐRE)
0,5 kg sertésnyelv
1 kis fej vöröshagyma
2 gerezd fokhagyma
ízlés szerint só, egész bors, babérlevél

A GOMBÓCHOZ
25 dkg Ella burgonya
5 dkg rétesliszt
1 db tojás
1 ek burgonyakeményítő
12 dkg tepertő
1 dkg vöröshagyma
1 gerezd fokhagyma
1 szál kakukkfű

A KÁPOSZTÁHOZ
50 dkg káposzta
1 dkg vaj
1 dkg vöröshagyma
0,5 dl fehérbor
5 dl alaplé
friss tárkony, só, bors

A MANGALICABŐRCHIPSHEZ
10 dkg sertésbőr
2 dkg szemes feketebors
1 babérlevél

AJÁNLOTT BOR
RÁSPI PINCÉSZET
Pinot Noir 2005

A nyelveket célszerű egy nappal korábban elkészíteni: ekkor a hagymákkal és a fűszerekkel ízesíteni vízben puhára főzzük. Még melegen lehúzuk a bőrét, majd a főzőlében hagyjuk kihűlni.

A gombóchoz a burgonyát a tálalás előtti napon héjában megfőzzük, és hidegen lehúzzuk. A túlrelészhez a tepertőt a hagymával és a fűszerekkel félhevítjük, majd az 1/3 részét pépesítjük, összekeverjük a maradékkal, és lehűtjük. A kihűlt főtt burgonyát lereszeljük, összekeverjük a liszttel, keményítővel, sóval, a tojással és borssal. Gombócokat formázunk a masszából, a középpe tepertőkrémet tesszük, a gombócokat jól összegyúrjuk, és gyöngyöző forró vízben kézre főzzük.

A káposztát vékony csíkokra vágjuk, és vajon, hagymával megfuttatjuk, majd sóval és borssal ízesítjük. Kevés fehérborral felöntjük, alaplével felöntjük, míg szinte az összes levét elfőtte. Ekkor felöntjük az alaplével és kézre párolva, frissítjük tárkonnyal.

Tálalásnál a tányérra helyezzük a káposztát, rá a gombócokat és a nyelvet. Tálalással díszíthetjük sertésbőrchips-szel: ehhez a bőrt abáléban (fűszeres botsal és babérlevéllel (rozsitett forró vízben) puhára főzük, leszárítjuk, majd egy kevés lével egyszerinűre ternmolizujük. Szűrőn átnyik, hűtőben megkeneszitjük, majd vékony lapokat üríink belőle, és forró, 200 fokos sütőben ropogós chipset készítünk belőle. A nyelvet ezzel tálaljuk.

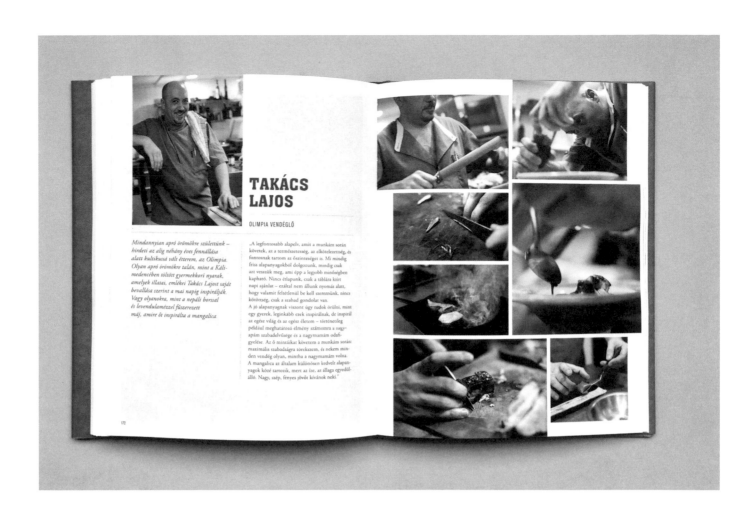

TAKÁCS LAJOS

OLIMPIA VENDÉGLŐ

Mindannyian apró örömökre születtünk – hirdeti az alig néhány éves fennállása alatt kultikussá vált étterem, az Olimpia. Olyan apró örömökre talán, mint a Káli-medencében töltött gyermekkori nyarak, amelyek illatai, emlékei Takács Lajost saját bevallása szerint a mai napig inspirálják. Vagy olyanokra, mint a nepáli borssal és levendulamézzel fűszerezett máj, amire őt inspirálta a mangalica.

„A legfontosabb alapelv, amit a munkám során követek, az a természetesség, az elkötelezettség, és fontosnak tartom az őszinteséget is. Mi mindig friss alapanyagokból dolgozunk, mindig csak azt vesszük meg, ami épp a legjobb minőségben kapható. Nincs étlapunk, csak a táblára kiírt napi ajánlat – ezáltal nem állunk nyomás alatt, hogy valamit feltétlenül be kell szereznünk, nincs kötöttség, csak a szabad gondolat van.

A jó alapanyagnak viszont úgy tudok örülni, mint egy gyerek, leginkább ezek inspirálnak, de inspirál az egész világ és az egész életem – történetileg például meghatározó élmény számomra a nagyapám szabadelvűsége és a nagymamám odafigyelése. Az ő mintáikat követem a munkám során: maximális szabadságra törekszem, és nekem minden vendég olyan, mintha a nagymamám volna.

A mangalica az általam különösen kedvelt alapanyagok közé tartozik, mert íze, az állaga egyedülálló. Nagy, szép, fényes jövőt kívánok neki."

SÁRKÖZI ÁKOS

BORKONYHA

A magyar konyhaművészet egyik legnagyobb reménységének tartják, pedig ő nem csinál mást, mint »egyszerű, de ízekben gazdag ételeket«. Alázata, felkészültsége és itt-ott megcsillanó gasztronómiai friskái (az olyanok, mint a fekete szaftol) a Borkonyhát a legjobb éttermek közé emelték. Sárközi Ákost pedig számos elismeréshez juttatták az elmúlt években.

„Gasztronómiai alapelvek nem igazán léteznek számomra – nekem az ízek és a formák határozzák meg az ételeimet. Az egyszerű, de ízekben gazdag ételeket kedvelem, ami pedig a formákat illeti, a színekkel együtt különös figyelmet kapnak nálam – ezek olykor a kiindulópontot is jelzik egy étel megalkotásánál. Magyarként mi más motiválna a konyhámban, mint az otthoni ízek? Az én esetemben a családi konyha, a családban szerzett gasztronómiai tapasztalat erőteljesen rányomja bélyegét a munkámra, ezek emlékei bukkannak fel minden ételemben. A személyes kapcsolat, kötődés a munkám más területein is fontos: napi kapcsolatban vagyok a termelőinkkel, tenyésztőinkkel, beszállítóinkkal, és személyesen kutatok a legjobb minőségű alapanyagok után. A mangalica számomra Magyarországot jelenti. Rendszeresen dolgozom vele, minden apró porcikájával, a fülétől a farkáig. Csak remélni merem, hogy a jó és állandó minőségű mangalicahús hamarosan mindenki számára elérhető lesz, és ezáltal hazánk egyik sikertörténetévé válhat. Nem kell mindig libamáj…"

Let's Have
a Snack

- **Design Agency**
  Patterns Digital Agency

- **Designer**
  Edoardo Biasini

- **Material**
  Burgo Papers Selena Green

- **Printing Technology**
  UV Varnishing

- **Size**
  170mm x 240mm

- **Completion**
  2014

- **Photo Credit**
  Edoardo Biasini

- **Publisher**
  Gallucci Editore

'Let's Have a Snack' (*Facciamo Merenda!*), by Miralda Colombo and Cecilia Viganò, revolves around the world's most desirable meal—the midday snack. The design brief called for a vintage theme that would hark back to a period when Italy's midday snack was commonly regarded as a necessity.

In line with this, the designer chose to use the former favorite Bruno Munari font New Caledonia for the titles and a playful Sauna font for the body copy, bearing in mind the book was meant to appeal to both adults and children (activities and puzzles appear alongside recipes).

The overall print color and texture achieved by using Burgo's Selena Green paper further contributed to the retro look—an early 1970s color palette and lined and squared exercise-book backgrounds enhanced the paper's texture. Furthermore, the book was created with round edges and a reduced size, and printed with a low contrast to simulate a vintage notepad. Indeed, a typographic grid allows the reader to make notes in the book's margins. Every chapter contains iconographic illustrations that were developed around a theme.

piatti caldo andante
tempi di preparazione 40 minuti (+ 2 ore di riposo)
tempi di cottura 20 minuti circa

Bracciali di pane e pomodoro condito

INGREDIENTI PER L'IMPASTO
400 g di farina "0" forte
100 g di semola di grano rimacinata
1 patata bollita e schiacciata
1 bustina di lievito madre essiccato
(o lievito di birra secco)
olio extravergine d'oliva
1 cucchiaino scarso di zucchero
1 cucchiaino di sale
acqua quanto basta

INGREDIENTI PER IL CONDIMENTO
pomodori freschi maturi
100 g di primo sale
origano
50 g di olive verdi
1 spicchio di aglio

Il "pane condito" è uno dei ricordi culinari dei miei viaggi in Sicilia (insieme agli arancini, ai cannoli, alla granita di corbezzolo e alla pasta con le sarde). Ho voluto riprodurre a casa questa ricetta semplice ma estremamente profumata d'estate, utilizzando la farcitura come ripieno di piccoli bracciali di pane "focaccioso", da mangiucchiare a piccoli morsi.

Comincia a impastare le farine con il lievito, la patata schiacciata, un paio di cucchiai di olio, un cucchiaino di zucchero e un bicchiere di acqua tiepida, nel quale avrai precedentemente sciolto un cucchiaino abbondante di sale. Lavora il tutto per una decina di minuti, se necessario aggiungi altra acqua. Fai lievitare la palla ottenuta in un luogo caldo per un paio d'ore.
Intanto taglia a pezzettini piccoli i pomodori, falli scolare eliminando l'acqua in eccesso, condiscili con un paio di cucchiai di olio, le olive ridotte a pezzetti piccoli, lo spicchio di aglio, che poi eliminerai, un cucchiaino di origano.
Ricava dall'impasto tante piccole porzioni da 30 g circa, stendile ciascuna in un rettangolo di circa 15-20 cm x 5 cm: metti al centro un cucchiaio di condimento, aggiungi dei pezzettini di primo sale, infine arrotola il rettangolo, chiudendo bene i due estremi. Unisci le due estremità del rotolino formando un cerchio, proprio come se fosse un bracciale. Appoggia infine su carta da forno. Procedi nello stesso modo col resto dell'impasto. Lascia lievitare i bracciali per quaranta minuti, poi spennellali con una salamoia fatta di tre parti di olio e una di acqua, spolverali con una manciata di origano fine. Puoi decorare la superficie aiutandoti con un coltello o con una forchetta: crea piccole strisce, rombi o altre forme.
Fai cuocere in forno preriscaldato a 200° per circa venti minuti.

101

La merenda dell'ABC

This cookbook contains favorite recipes from employees at investment company Garantum; these employees are no chefs, but they are specialists in combining components to create a successful whole. With this book, Garantum wanted to create a sense of what the company is about and to share this with potential clients.

With a Sense of Timing

- **Design Agency**
  Alinder Design

- **Designer**
  Sara Alinder

- **Material**
  Uncoated Paper 150gsm
  Amber Graphic

- **Printing Technology**
  White Foil Embossing

- **Size**
  175mm x 245mm

- **Completion**
  2015

- **Photo Credit**
  Sara Alinder

- **Publisher**
  Alinder Design

The title of the book is all about the importance of timing in cooking. To be able to succeed in the kitchen, a good knowledge of the ingredients and a sense of timing are required: a few degrees higher or a few minutes longer can make meat dry or vegetables too soft. This book is about cooking things in an optimal way.

Alinder Design won the Swedish Publishing Prize (Svenska Publishing-Priset), one of the most prestigious publishing awards in Sweden, for both the design and content of this book.

West Masuria

- **Design Agency**
  Studio Polkadot

- **Material**
  130gsm Munken Pure
  Rough Paper

- **Size**
  176mm x 250mm

- **Completion**
  2014

- **Photo Credit**
  Łukasz Filak

Poland's West Masuria Tourism Cluster published this book to promote the region's local food. Members of the organization provided recipes of their favorite dishes for the publication. The design of the book references a notebook from a tour, and each spread is designed to reflect the character of the places the dishes come from. This is achieved partly through the typography used—more sophisticated typefaces are used on pages that relate to expensive restaurants, while handwriting expresses the informal character of agricultural farms. Marta Potoczek was responsible for the book's photography and styling.

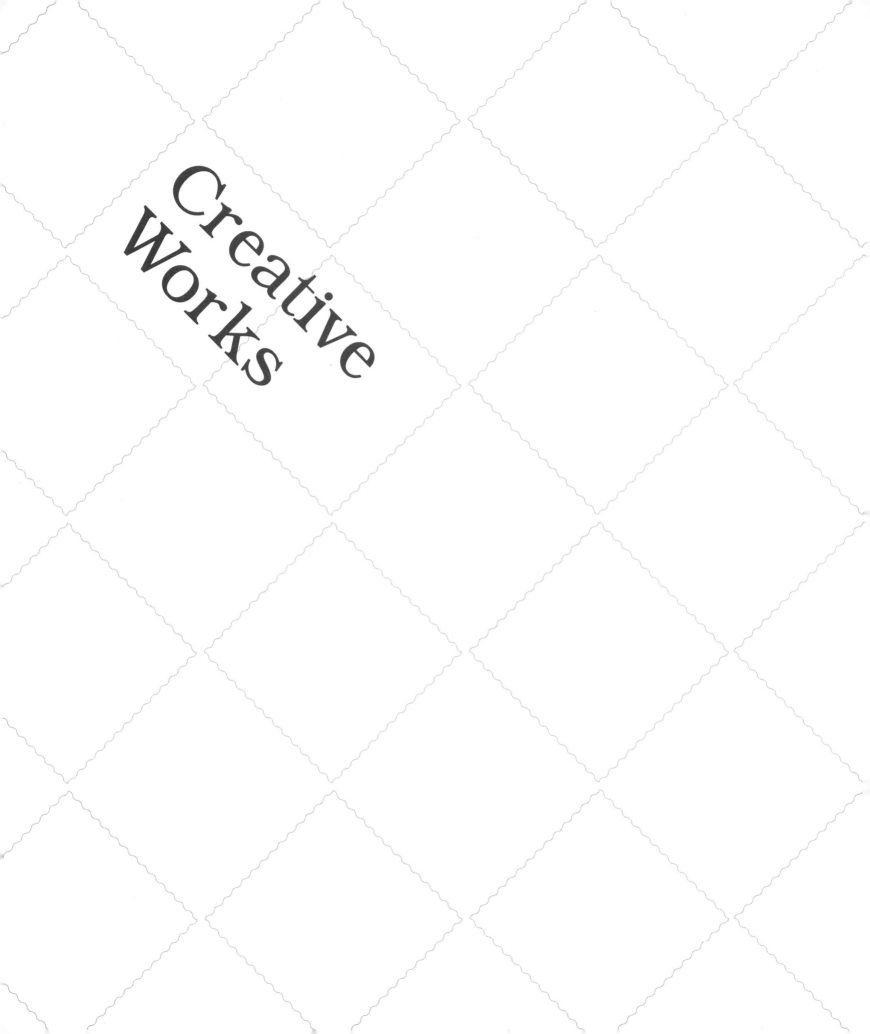

Creative
Works

A Feast for the Eyes

By Evi O.

The joy of eating is probably the one unifying pleasure every human can relate to, and food is an important way for people to connect. Aiding these connections, cookbooks used to be a collection of dozens of recipes, often without photography or illustrations, things that would be used and shared every day. More recently, however, cookbooks have become much more than this—they're now often objects of desire, 'almost-art' objects, and lavishly produced publications grace the shelves of most bookstores.

The finest examples feature the best of print production, moving cookbooks into a specialized illustrated book niche. From Salvador Dali's *Les Dîners de Gala* to Julia Child's *Mastering the Art of French Cooking*, cookbooks cater to both functional and recreational needs, claiming a must-have status on a kitchen bench or coffee table.

Celebrity chefs (Jamie Oliver, Heston Blumenthal and the like) and the increase in TV cooking shows (like *MasterChef*) have contributed hugely to the amount of commercial cookbooks flooding the market. Then there's the blogging community with its own independent cookbooks. Personally, I am both overwhelmed and excited every time I go to my local bookshop to see all of the new titles.

This boom has created the coveted role of a specialized designer, who has a range of skills beyond that of just graphic design. The layout, design, photography and print finishes of a cookbook have never been more important. Audiences these days need to feel they are getting something more than just a collection of new recipes. Why else would they buy a new cookbook if they can download an electronic version on their iPad? The physical book has to demand to be treasured, not just for the text, but for the visual elements that combine to create a thing of beauty that readers will cherish.

I was thrilled when the publisher of this book mentioned that there would be a creative cookbook section, featuring works that push the boundaries of traditional design and make a functional cookbook stand out from the rest.

The following sections cover some of the rules a cookbook designer considers, follows and sometimes disregards in order to create something that breaks the mold. Note that all comments are based on my own professional experience of working as a cookbook designer in one of the most prestigious global publishing houses for over eight years.

Concept to Final Results

I find the most creative cookbooks often apply one little (or big) idea and religiously stick to it with every single execution of format, layout, typography and photography. The designers of these books are not afraid to break the grid, but they also keep in mind the unified flow/look of the concept as a whole, which can result in a dynamic package that offers surprises on every page.

A stellar example of this is *Tofu* (p104), a beautifully produced book that illustrates qualities of tofu by using different paper types. It is also meticulously wrapped in cloth and presented in a traditional wooden tofu mold, mimicking the real thing.

A much more commercial example is *Greek* (p152). Celebrity chef George Calombaris' Greek heritage and his passion for street art were the design's starting points. Bold typography, stencil art and gritty food styling are harmoniously married in the form of a functional cookbook. The addition of a sticker sheet for readers to create their own feast reflects the cheeky personality of the author, elevating the book to 'not your average celebrity chef cookbook' status.

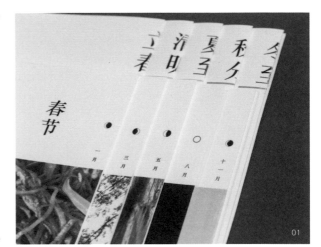

I'd also like to highlight *Seasons in Singapore* (p210/Figure 01), which, among other design elements, uses the phases of the moon as an icon that navigates the reader through a series of seasonal dishes. Similarly, *Cooking with Colors* (p136) visually translates the concept of a harmonious Chinese diet theory, which advocates incorporating food from five different color categories into every meal. The designer of this book diligently used matching color palettes throughout to highlight the food/color groups in the layout design. Choosing these different elements—the moon phases and color coding—are essential design decisions that form a crucial part of the reader's understanding of the content and help them navigate the book.

01

Format, Stock and Finishes— the Book as an Object

The dimension, weight and finishes of a book are key to ensuring a successful and well-rounded final package. A tall book implies sophistication, a hand-bound spine radiates craftsmanship, and book designers will opt for uncoated stock if they don't want a heavy book. Detailed attention to all these factors will add interaction value for readers, presenting contents in a more engaging way.

02

Tea-Hee (p124/Figure 02) successfully communicates the slow process of tea making and the calmness of enjoying a cup of tea through quiet, yet informative design. Combined with its hand-sewn binding finish, this results in an intimate package.

Both *Sweets* (p164/Figure 03) and *Cooking Game* (p142) push the traditional book format, with end results that don't look like a book and surely stand out on bookshop shelves. It is important to think outside the box, while not forgetting the functionality of the physical object.

03

Layout—the Art of Recipe Design

This topic is probably the core of good cookbook design. A functional recipe design that is easy to follow, read and use in the kitchen is always first priority when I tackle a cookbook. It's important to consider what style of cooking the author has—for example, some authors have long ingredient lists, some very short methods. Then there's potential extra information to include, such as tips, allergy ratings, calorie counts and other details that vary from one cookbook to the next and steer the direction of layout design.

While a cookbook often feels templated, recipe layout design is an art of its own. The case studies presented in this section showcase some of the best examples of how to cater to this challenge—and push it a little bit further—presenting a unique reading/ cooking experience.

Highlights include *All about Porridge* (p128), which features pictures of ingredients, saving amateur cooks from having to Google what particular grains look like. *Bbang*'s (p108) addition of handwritten annotations pulls the reader in while giving cooking tips, adding another layer to its recipe design.

Cookbook for Children (p182) cleverly showcases the before and after shot of pureed recipes, avoiding pages of what could otherwise have been repetitive puree shots. *Dalocska's Bakery* (p116) generously illustrates every single step of each recipe's method, which would prove very helpful for bakers with little knowledge. These illustrations have both a decorative and practical function.

Photography, Illustration and Typography

When working on illustrated books, a book designer will often be doing more than just graphic design—they might also be involved with art direction, image retouching, illustration, and sometimes even styling and content production. There's so much more to illustrated books than meets the eye.

A book designer is often involved from the very beginning of visual conception, allowing careful planning of every single design execution. Photography, illustration and typography, or a combination of all three of these disciplines, can be used as much more than just decorative elements. Many of the case studies in this section demonstrate how a book's visual elements are just as important as its text, highlighting how crucial design development is to the feel and tone of the overall cookbook.

I'd like to highlight a book I designed: *T2—The Book* (p144), a comprehensive publication about tea varieties, processing and drinking produced by the global tea brand T2. The company's aim was to create the most exciting book about tea ever, which is in line with its sleek branding and youthful approach to the centuries-old subject matter. Working collaboratively with a team of photographers and illustrators, we made sure each page had its own surprises, featuring dynamic images to balance the no-fuss layout design. Tea leaves are peppered throughout the book to add

decorative elements, while photography is included alongside information design elements. This book was a great exercise in content collaboration and creation, where combining the talents of many resulted in a unique, unified execution.

'The Luitpold' (*Das Luitpold*, p120/Figure 04) is both a coffee table book and cookbook about Munich's famous Cafe Luitpold. Narratives are accompanied by thoughtfully produced images and hand lettering, in keeping with the café's visual identity. Portraits of chefs and customers coupled with behind-the-scenes and architecture shots go beyond the traditional food-on-plate photography, providing readers with an atmospheric and visual narrative of what it's like being in the café.

What follows in this chapter makes me excited as a book designer. In this digital age, all the case studies presented following demonstrate that the humble, physical cookbook can, and will, stand on its own— and that buying another bookshelf is justifiable.

04

Evi O. is a book designer, art director and artist based in Sydney, Australia. She has worked in the book publishing industry for almost a decade, specializing in illustrated books.

Tofu

- **Designer**
  Cheryl Chong

- **Material**
  Handmade Tofu Paper,
  Watercolor Paper, Wooden
  Box Casing

- **Size**
  180mm x 280mm

- **Completion**
  2013

Tofu is a recipe book that hopes to inspire healthy eating, especially in our hectic daily life where fast and unhealthy food is so prevalent. This is an exploration into a healthier lifestyle through tofu, and is based upon the central concepts of white and emptiness, which can be traced to Buddhist Zen and Taoist ideas.

The packaging is designed to resemble a traditional wooden tofu mold, and opening the lid reveals the book wrapped in cotton cloth, creating an impression of freshly made tofu. Textured pages are incorporated within sections of the book to reflect different qualities of tofu. For example, some layered, hand-torn paper is a subtle representation of ripples created by the stirring of boiling soymilk; this was inspired by the poem 'Ode to Tofu' by a renowned female poet of the Yuan dynasty, Zheng Yunduan (1327–1356). Other examples include a thin piece of tracing paper that was crushed and dyed with yellow food coloring to look like tofu skin, and paper that is handmade using tofu.

These design elements successfully express the intangible qualities of tofu through tangible materials.

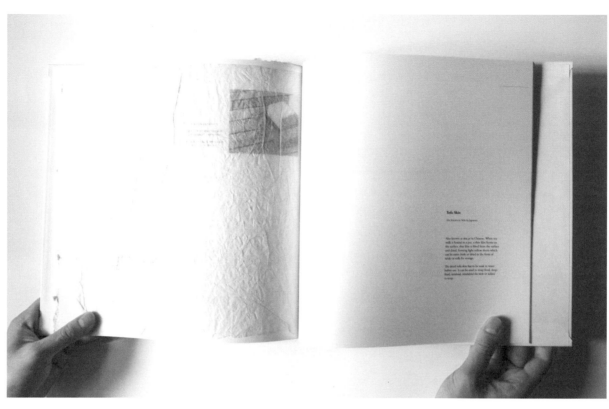

Tofu Making Essentials
豆腐製作必備

Essential Equipment

Pot

Choose a big pot about two to three
times the amount of water that is being
used, for boiling the soybean liquid.
Another smaller pot to hold the soy
milk in. Using a nonstick pot will make
cleaning easier.

Blender

Regular counter top blender, not the
hand-held immersion kind. Renders the
soaked beans and water to silky thick
texture in no time. Food processor can be
an alternative.

Large Colander or Mesh Strainer

Choose a colander that is a little larger
than the largest pot you are using to boil
the soy milk, so that it fits inside but
extends over the rim.

Tofu Mold

Choose a tofu pressing box made of wood
or plastic or a Japanese colander (zaru).
Wooden ones are larger and have a
removable bottom for easy unmolding.
Japanese tofu molds are beautifully
crafted and can be expensive, but worth
purchasing if you regularly make tofu.

Pressing Cloth

Prepare a large piece of cotton cloth to
squeeze the soy milk with. A big piece of
light weight unbleached muslin or cotton
dishtowel will work.

Mold Liner Cloth

Use either the fabric which c...
mold or a lightweight fabr...
or unbleached muslin...
3 times the size of...

Bbang

- **Designer**
  Joy Han

- **Material**
  Bright Colorful Paper

- **Size**
  213mm x 318mm

- **Photo Credit**
  Joy Han

Bbang is a cookbook that presents traditional Korean bread recipes, stories, photography, and personal interviews that were compiled in order to help younger Korean-Americans remember their cultural roots. The designer, Joy Han, was born and raised in America and grew up with American culture, which made her forget her Korean heritage.

With this in mind, Han created this book with a focus on Korean bread. An organic and free-flowing style of typography is used to reflect the hand-made bread recipes. The handwritten font style also represents how she would imagine herself jotting down notes if she was cooking these recipes from scratch. Han wanted the reader to fully understand and experience the bread-making process, to feel as though they are on the scene with the baker. However, she still tried to maintain a balance between the structured and the free-form.

Street art also inspired the typography. It goes well with the Korean bread theme, because many of the recipes in the book are the best and most famous street foods in Korea.

Moon Shaped Rice Cake

Songpyeon is a traditional Korean food made of glutinous rice. It is a type of ddeok, consisting of small rice cakes traditionally eaten during the Korean autumn harvest festival, Chuseok. They have become a popular symbol of traditional Korean culture. Songpyeons are moon-shaped rice cakes that contain different kinds of sweet or semi-sweet fillings, such as sesame seeds and honey, sweet red bean paste, and chestnut paste steamed over a layer of pine needles, which gives them the fragrant smell of fresh pine trees. They were made into various shapes with the participation of family members and were often exchanged between neighbors.

(Song-pyeon)

THE FILLING:

The Best Part

.5 CUP of ROASTED SESAME SEEDS
2 TBS of SUGAR (ADJUST TO YOUR TASTE)
Pinch of SALT
1 TBS of HONEY

sesame seeds
sugar
honey
salt

matcha
green TEA
powder

Rasberries

rice powder

Kobacha
SQUASH

Blueberry
JUICE

PINK RICE CAKE:

With Raspberries

2 CUPS of FROZEN RICE FLOUR
4 TBS of RASPBERRY JUICE
.5 CUP of FROZEN RASPBERRIES FINELY PUREED
1/2 CUP of BOILING WATER

YELLOW RICE CAKE:

With Kobacha Squash

2 CUPS of FROZEN RICE FLOUR
1/3 CUP of COOKED & STEAMING KOBOCHA
2 TBS of BOILING WATER

PURPLE RICE CAKE:

With Blueberries

2 CUPS of FROZEN RICE FLOUR
4 TBS of HOT BLUEBERRY JUICE
.5 CUP of FROZEN BLUEBERRIES FINELY PUREED
1/2 CUP of BOILING WATER

GREEN RICE CAKE:

With Green Tea

2 CUPS of FROZEN RICE FLOUR
2 TBS of MATCHA GREEN TEA POWDER
5 TBS of BOILING WATER

WHITE RICE CAKE:

The Original

2 CUSP of FROZEN RICE FLOUR
4 TBS plus 1 or 2 TSP OF BOILING WATER

SONG-PYEON 36

MOON SHAPED RICE CAKE 37

This book is dedicated to my family for helping me find who I really am and where I come from.

가족
(ga-jok)

꼬과배
(kkwa-bae-g

Why Bread?

THE RICE CAKE:
The Chewy Goodness

1 CUP *of* SWEET RICE FLOUR
1/4 TSP *of* SALT
3/4 CUP *of* WATER

sweet
RICE
FLOUR

salt
+
sugar

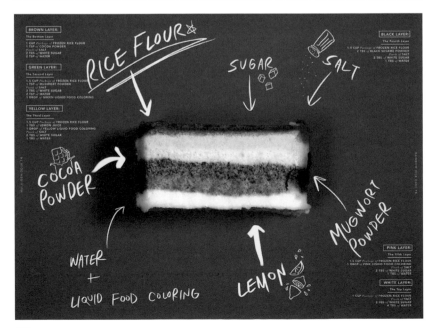

BROWN LAYER:
The Bottom Layer

GREEN LAYER:
The Second Layer

YELLOW LAYER:
The Third Layer

BLACK LAYER:
The Fourth Layer

PINK LAYER:
The Fifth Layer

WHITE LAYER:
The Top Layer

RICE FLOUR

SUGAR

SALT

COCOA
POWDER

MUGWORT
POWDER

WATER
+
LIQUID FOOD COLORING

LEMON

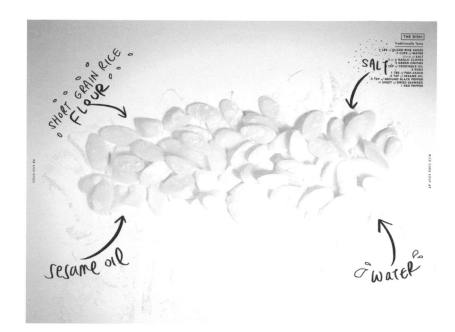

Traditionally Tasty

1 LBS of SLICED RICE CAKES
7 CUPS of WATER
Pinch of SALT
4 GARLIC CLOVES
3 GREEN ONIONS
1 TSP of VEGETABLE OIL
2 EGGS
1 TBS of FISH SAUCE
2 TSP of SESAME OIL
.5 TSP of GROUND BLACK PEPPER
1 SHEET of DRIED SEAWEED
1 RED PEPPER

SHORT GRAIN RICE FLOUR

SALT

sesame oil

WATER

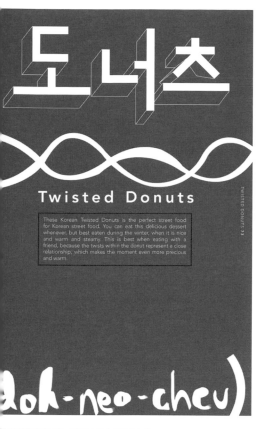

도너츠

Twisted Donuts

These Korean Twisted Donuts is the perfect street food for Korean street food. You can eat this delicious dessert whenever, but best eaten during the winter, when it is nice and warm and steamy. This is best when eating with a friend, because the twists within the donut represent a close relationship, which makes the moment even more precious and warm.

(oh-neo-cheu)

LARGE BOWL
STRAINER

FISH-SHAPED PAN
MIXING SPOON

THE COATING:

Great Texture

1/2 CUP of ROASTED SOYBEAN POWDER
sprinkle of SUGAR

Roasted soybean powder

MUGWORT POWDER

DRY INGREDIENTS:

6 RICE CRACKERS

4 CUPS of DRIED & POPPED RICE
2 TBS of WHITE SUGAR
Pinch of SALT
Sprinkle a PACKET of ORIGINAL GELATIN

RICE FLOUR

corn syrup

SUGAR

Gelatin

LIQUID INGREDIENTS:

4 RICE CRACKERS

1 CUP of CORN SYRUP
1/2 CUP of WATER

The Puglia
in a Plate

- **Designers**
  Alessandro Santoro,
  Dario Miale, Pierfrancesco
  Annicchiarico

- **Material**
  Jacket: 300gsm Mattcoated
  Paper;
  Text: 150gsm Mattcoated
  Paper

- **Printing Technology**
  UV Varnish

- **Size**
  220mm x 220mm

- **Photo Credit**
  Dario Miale

'The Puglia in a Plate' (*La Puglia in un Piatto*) presents 60 traditional recipes within its 170-plus pages from the southern Italian region of Puglia. It's the result of a study that sought to explore the relationship between a meal and the plate or vessel it's served on/in, and aims to extend the concept of food to a broader sensory experience.

Ceramic tableware is the main source of inspiration for much of the book's content and design. The plate ('piatto')

is the main protagonist, playing the double role as a thing of both beauty and function, and being the ideal medium to represent the unique identity of Puglian cuisine.

Graphic design group Usopposto made this project a journey to savor through the use of different stylistic figures; one of its aims was to enrich the literary scene that deals with Puglian gastronomy.

150   Cupeta

64   Peppered mussels

38   Rabbit with vegetables

The main aim of this work was to create an easy-to-use, illustrated and unusual recipe book. The designer's vintage-style illustrations are the main feature of the book; they guide the reader step-by-step through each recipe's method. Recipes for muffins, cakes, slices, quiches and other baked goods are all accompanied by her delightful hand drawings, graphic elements, and photographs of the finished products. Each recipe's spread is created in a different style and mood, and tells a different visual story.

Dalocska's Bakery

- **Designer**
  Kiss Lenke 'Dalocska'

- **Material**
  120gsm Gloss

- **Size**
  153mm x 196mm

- **Completion**
  2014

- **Photo Credit**
  Kiss Lenke 'Dalocska'

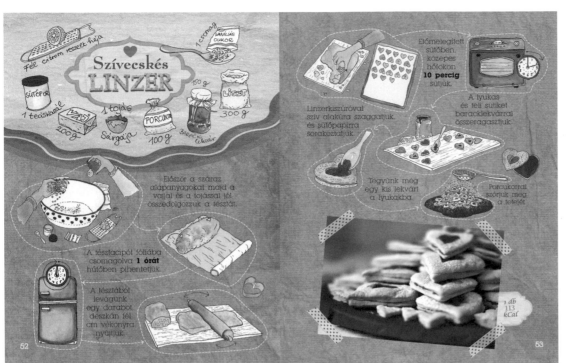

Szívecskés LINZER

Fél citrom reszelt héja · 1 csomag VANÍLIÁS CUKOR

SÜTŐPOR · VAJ 200 g · 1 teáskanál · 1 tojás · Sárgája · PORCUKOR 100 g · BARACKLEKVÁR · LISZT 300 g · 150 g

Először a száraz alapanyagokat majd a vajjal és a tojással jól összedolgozzuk a tésztát.

A tésztacipót fóliába csomagolva **1 órát** hűtőben pihentetjük.

A tésztából levágunk egy darabot, deszkán fél cm vékonyra nyújtjuk.

Linzerkiszúróval szív alakúra szaggatjuk, és sütőpapírra sorakoztatjuk.

Előmelegített sütőben, közepes hőfokon **10 percig** sütjük.

A lyukas és teli sütiket baracklekvárral összeragasztjuk.

Tegyünk még egy kis lekvárt a lyukakba.

Porcukorral szórjuk meg a tetejét.

1 db 113 kCal

52 · 53

Spenótos Quiche

Hozzávalók

só
200 g finomliszt
2-3 gerezd fokhagyma
100 g krémsajt
szerecsendió
100 g vaj · 2-3 ek víz
(olívaolaj)
200 g sajt · 500 g spenót
3 tojás · 200 ml tejszín
fehér bors

A lisztet, a sót és a felkockázott puha vajat morzsold össze.

Utána kanalanként add hozzá a vizet, majd gyúrd össze a tésztát.

Letakarva, legalább 30 percre tedd a hűtőbe.

A spenótot borssal, fokhagymával, sóval, kevés olíva olajon párold meg.

28

Kakaós csiga

kakaó
30 ml tej
150 g zsírszegény túró
150 g teljes kiőrlésű liszt
1/2 csomag sütőpor
60 g porcukor
3 ek olaj
só

1. A túrót, cukrot, sót, tejet tegyük egy tálba és az olajat fokozatosan adagolva keverjük alaposan el.

2. Hozzáadjuk a sütőporral elkevert lisztet.

3. Lisztezett felületen átgyúrjuk és téglalap formájúra nyújtjuk. A porcukrot, kis olajat, kakaót összekeverjük és megkenjük vele a tészta tetejét.

4. Feltekerjük, és kb. 1-2 cm vastag szeletekre vágjuk.

5. Sütőpapírral bélelt tepsibe helyezzük és előmelegített sütőben 15 perc alatt megsütjük.

Sütési hőfok: 180 °C
Sütés ideje: 15 perc
1 db **75** kCal

ENJOY!

Kakaós Csiga

A tejszínt, krémsajtot, tojást, reszelt sajtot, sót, borsot, reszelt szerecsendiót egy tálban keverd össze.

Kivajazott formába a kinyújtott tésztát nyomkodd bele, és a tésztát szurkáld meg villával.

Sütőpapírral lefedve, babbal a tetején süsd előmelegített sütőben 15 percig, és míg 5 percig papír nélkül.

Terítsd szét a spenóton a sajtos keveréket, majd 30 perc alatt süsd aranybarnára.

180 °C

1 szelet 370 kCal

29

Citromos Joghurtos Muffin
meggyel

Hozzávalók:
26 dkg liszt
1 ék sütőpor
1/2 kk szódabikarbóna
1 csomag vaníliás cukor
1/2 dl kókuszzsír (olaj)
2 dl citromos joghurt
1 citrom, 2 tojás
12 szem meggy
15 dkg xilit

liszt

xilit cukor

1. Egy tálban keverjük el a sütőporral a lisztet, a cukrokat, szódabikarbónát, citrom reszelt héját.

2. Másik tálban a tojásokat keverjük el a joghurttal, kókuszzsírral, citrom levével, majd adjuk hozzá a lisztes keverékhez.

3. A tésztát a muffin formákba kanalazzuk, 3/4-ig töltjük, tetejére magozott meggyet nyomkodunk, és szép aranybarnára sütjük.

Porcukorral díszíthetjük

Sütési hőfok: 180 °C
Sütés ideje: 20-25 perc

1 db 197 kCal

12

13

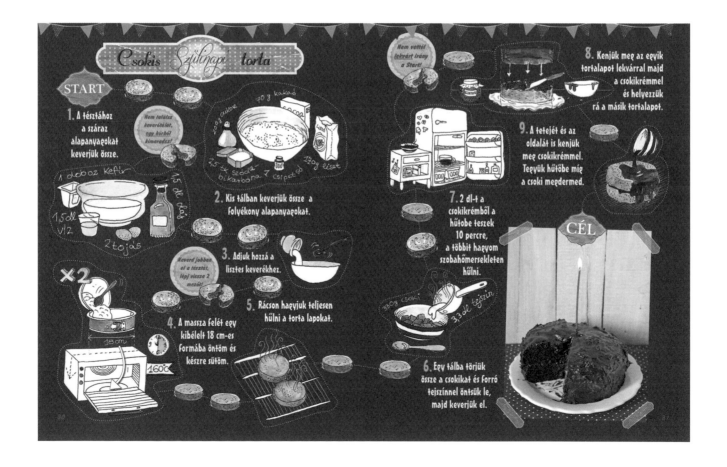

Csokis Szülinapi torta

START

1. A tésztához a száraz alapanyagokat keverjük össze.

Nem tufálsz keverőlut, egy kürből kimaradsz!

200 g cukor
70 g kakaó
cocoa
170 g liszt
1,5 tk szóda bikarbóna 7 csipetsó

1 doboz kefir
1,5 dl olaj
1,5 dl víz
2 tojás

2. Kis tálban keverjük össze a folyékony alapanyagokat.

×2

3. Adjuk hozzá a lisztes keverékhez.

Keverd jobban el a tésztát, lépj vissza 2 mezőt!

4. A massza felét egy kibélelt 18 cm-es formába öntöm és készre sütöm.

18 cm
160°C

5. Rácson hagyjuk teljesen hűlni a torta lapokat.

6. Egy tálba törjük össze a csokikat és forró tejszínnel öntsük le, majd keverjük el.

300 g csoki
3,3 dl tejszín

7. 2 dl-t a csokikrémből a hűtőbe teszek 10 percre, a többit hagyom szobahőmérsékleten hűlni.

Nem vetted lekvárt irány a Start!

8. Kenjük meg az egyik tortalapot lekvárral majd a csokikrémmel és helyezzük rá a másik tortalapot.

9. A tetejét és az oldalát is kenjük meg csokikrémmel. Tegyük hűtőbe míg a csoki megdermed.

CÉL

119

The Luitpold

- **Design Agency**
  Rose Pistola GmbH

- **Designers**
  Maria Fischer,
  Frank Weidenfelder

- **Material**
  Paper, Cardboard

- **Size**
  225mm x 290mm

- **Completion**
  2012

- **Photo Credit**
  Matthias Haslauer

'The Luitpold' (*Das Luitpold*) is both a coffee table book and a cookbook. It tells the story of Munich's famous Cafe Luitpold since 1888 and of German coffeehouse culture, describing the extraordinary habits of people in the 19th century. Three hundred pages are filled with anecdotes and more than 40 gourmet food recipes. Text, images, hand lettering and copperplate collages—developed as part of the design concept to be recognizable elements from Cafe Luitpold's visual identity—combine to create a visually opulent rhythm.

IN DER
BACK
STUBE

*Zaubern mit Chefkonditor
Albert Ziegler*

Wie oft und je wird in den Arbeitsräumen über dem Café alles mit der
Hand gemacht. Kuchen, Torten und die 60 Pralinearten, die es im Luitpold gibt.
Dazu gehören der Tagesträffel, das knusperknäckige Nougatmünchen oder
Monte Rosa, ein kompaktes Miniaturwunder aus Buttercrème.

Bombieren

Dünngehauchte Hippenblätter, filigran
gefärmte Marzipanknospen, ein
liebevoll postuliertes Brezison – das
Konditorhandwerk verlangt künstlerisches
Fingispitz. Da steht man sich zartbesaitete
Virtuosen der Teigbehandlung vor, die mit
viel Hingabe und vor allem traulich vor
sich hin werkeln. Und dann das: bombieren,
dressieren. Die Sprache der Konditoren
ist derart martialisch, da kann man es mit
der Angst kriegen. Warum muss man eine
Bombe benützen, um zu beschreiben, dass
man eine süße Masse in eine Halbkugel
füllt? Warum wird Buttercrème dressiert,
sich halbwüt in Form gebracht? Auch den
Teig tut es am Ende weh, wenn man ihn
schlägt. Der Sahne geht es da nicht besser.

Wenn Albert Ziegler sich an das Kompo-
nieren einer neuen Praline macht, rührt
er in seinem Topf 100 Gramm Kuvertüre
1000 Gramm Sahne und zwei Kilogramm
Kuvertüre an – und experimentiert dann
mit Zutaten wie Kardamom, Chilipulver,
Champagner, Mandarinenzesten,
Fondantzucker, Kakaobohnengranulat und
Kakaobutter. Dabei entstehen kleine
Wunderwerke, die jede Sünde wert sind.

Baumkuchen

Der Baumkuchen ist der König aller Kuchen. Und das, wo man ihn am Spieß dreht wie ein Spanferkel. Das heißt, man gießt mit dem Schöpflöffel immer wieder neue Teigschichten auf den sich drehenden Spieß. Die backen dann vor sich hin, sodass – wie bei einem Baum – Jahresringe entstehen. Die lange Backzeit macht den Baumkuchen sehr haltbar und ermöglicht dadurch auch den Export nach Japan. Das ist wichtig. Denn in Japan findet man an jeder Ecke Baumkuchen. Die Japaner sind ganz verrückt danach. Einige schreiben sogar Blogs über Baumkuchen. Die kann der normale Mitteleuropäer zwar nicht lesen wegen der vielen japanischen Schriftzeichen, aber er kann sich an den schönen bunten Bildern erfreuen.

Konditormeister Albert Ziegler fing 1978 als Lehrling im Luitpold an, seit 2001 leitet er die Backstube. „Hier wird noch wie vor hundert Jahren gearbeitet“, sagt er, „ohne Fertigprodukte."

RAGOUT FIN

Die Zwiebel schälen und das Lorbeerblatt mit den Nelken darauf feststecken. In einem Topf 2 l Wasser mit der gespickten Zwiebel, den Wacholderbeeren, den Pfefferkörnern und ½ TL Salz aufkochen. Das Kalbfleisch einlegen und darin etwa 30 Minuten köcheln, bis es auf den Punkt genau gegart ist. Dann aus dem Sud nehmen und auf einem Teller zum Abkühlen beiseitestellen, den Sud aufheben. Das abgekühlte Fleisch in 5–8 mm große Würfel schneiden.

In einem Topf etwas Butter zerlassen und das Mehl darin anschwitzen. Mit Sahne, Weißwein und ½ l Kochsud zu einer homogenen Sauce aufgießen, aufkochen und die Weißweinsauce mit Zitronensaft, Salz, Pfeffer und Zucker abschmecken.

Die Waldpilze säubern und trocken abreiben, evtl. zerkleinern, die Schalotten schälen und in feine Würfel schneiden und beides in einer Pfanne in etwas Butter goldbraun anbraten.

Die Blätterteigpastetchen im Ofen bei 120 °C (Umluft 100 °C) erwärmen. Kurz vor dem Anrichten die Kalbfleischwürfel in die Weißweinsauce geben und darin aufkochen. Den Topf vom Herd ziehen und die geschlagene Sahne unterheben. Das Ragout in die Pastetchen füllen und die Waldpilze darübergeben.

ZUTATEN
für 4 Personen

1 Zwiebel
1 Lorbeerblatt
2 Gewürznelken
2 Wacholderbeeren
½ TL ganze Pfefferkörner
Salz
500 g Kalbfleisch
(aus der Schulter)
ca. 50 g Butter
50 g Mehl
200 g Sahne
5 EL Weißwein
Saft von 1 Zitrone
Pfeffer aus der Mühle
Zucker
200 g gemischte Waldpilze
2 Schalotten
4 kleine Blätterteigpasteten
(beim Bäcker oder Café
Luitpold vorbestellen)
etwas geschlagene Sahne

Tea-Hee

- **Designer**
  Jiani Lu

- **Material**
  Paperboard, Canvas Fabric,
  Paper

- **Size**
  148mm x 210mm

- **Completion**
  2013

Tea-Hee is a playful and lighthearted hand-bound book designed to be an informal reference guide for tea lovers. It introduces readers to the world of tea and its craft through chapters that paint a picture about the culture and craft of tea-making. A friendly and approachable tone is achieved through the use of inviting colors and organic lines. This does not compromise the technical information, however, which is enhanced by a systematic visual approach involving hard-edged illustrations and vector-based infographics.

The craftsmanship involved in producing the book was inspired by the art of tea making itself, a slow process that calls for patience and a hands-on approach. It features a handmade hardcover of canvas fabric and illustration board, and is coptic bound with four signatures.

All about Porridge

- **Designer**
  Eugenia Tynna

- **Size**
  170mm x 290mm

- **Completion**
  2013

The main idea of this project was to create a recipe book that focuses on different porridges (grains), especially as it's rare to find a book that concentrates on this one food topic. Each of the book's several sections introduces one kind of grain, beginning with a short history of the grain's origin, followed by recipes showing the different ways to cook it.

One of the difficulties encountered by the designer, Eugenia Tynna, was how to take good-quality photos without any professional tools (lights, soft boxes, professional cameras, and so on). She overcame this challenge by building a small home studio using chairs, lamps and other domestic items, and ended up enjoying the process.

однорічний кущ родини бобових, що вирощується задля лінзоподібного насіння. Рослина сягає до 60 см заввишки, насіння росте в стручках, зазвичай
з двома насінинами в кожному. Плід - біб. Насіння пласке, лінзоподібне, забарвлення від жовтого до чорного (в культурі переважають сорти зеленого,
червоного, та коричневого забарвлення).

Як готувати сочевицю

Коричнева сочевиця, що має горіховий присмак, найбільш поширена
в Європі й США, де з неї готують супи з овочами та травами. Червона
сочевиця хороша тим, що на її приготування витрачається мінімум часу -
10-15 хвилин. Якщо поварити червону сочевицю довше, то вийде смачна
каша. «Білуга» - це найменший сочевичний сорт, чорні круглі боби якого
насправді нагадують білугова ікру. Пюї - ароматна чорно-зелена сочевиця.
Своєю назвою вона зобов'язана імені французького міста, де її вивели. Ця
сочевиця хороша для салатів, так як довго не розварюється. Кольори сочевиці розрізняються часом приготування: зелена – готується трохи довше,
але зате практично не розварюється. Червона і коричнева варяться набага-
то швидше: опущена в окріп, така сочевиця звариться за 20-25 хвилин.
Сочевиця, на відміну від своїх родичів гороху і квасолі, не потребує замочування. При варінні її не солять, як і всі бобові, так як сіль сповільнить
процес. Перед тим, як почати приготування сочевиці, її потрібно перебра-
ти, промити в декількох водах. Варять, додавши в два рази більше води: на
склянку сочевиці – 2 склянки води. У процесі варіння необхідно декілька
раз перешкодити сочевицю.

САЛАТ
з сочевицею та м'ятою

1. Сочевицю покласти у невелику каструлю, додати часник і залити в три рази
більшим обсягом холодної води. Довести до кипіння. Додати кілька гілочок
м'яти, зменшити вогонь і залишити варитися під покришкою 30 хвилин.
2. Злити воду, вийняти часник і м'яту, покласти сочевицю назад у теплу каструлю, заправити оливковою олією і соком лимону.
3. Додати розтертий сухий чилі і порубану м'яту та спеції.
4. Подавати теплою, з листям зеленого салату, молодим шпинатом, зимовими
овочами: морквою, молодим буряком або цукіні, попередньо приготувавши їх
в духовці і заправленими оливковою олією і лимоном.

СОЧЕВИЦЯ
з помідорами

1. Сочевицю залити холодною водою, вимочити протягом 4-5 годин.
2. Цибулю порізати кубиками, помідори - шматочками. Обсмажити цибулю в
олії до золотистого кольору, додати помідори і тушкувати 2 хвилини.
3. До помідорів з цибулею додати сочевицю, влити склянку води і тушкувати
на маленькому вогні під закритою покришкою протягом 45 хвилин, доливаючи
води за необхідністю. До страви додати спеції, влити лимонний сік і тушкувати
ще 5 хвилин. Подавати, притрусивши зеленню петрушки.

ПЛОВ
з сочевицею та ізюмом

1. Промийти рис і сочевицю. Поставити їх варитися в різних каструлях у під-
соленій воді. Рис - на 15 хвилин, сочевицю - на 20 хвилин. Промити і викласти.
2. Нарізати цибулю кільцями і обсмажити у невеликій кількості олії. Добавити
до цибулі фарш та обсмажувати 10 хвилин. Влити у сковорідку півсклянки
гарячої води і продовжити тушкувати на середньому вогні (без покришки) до
того моменту, як вода випаровується.
3. Фініки очистити від шкірки та кісточок.
4. На дно казану налийти трошки олії, викласти половину рису, додайти 1/4
склянки гарячої води, потім м'ясо, сочевицю, ізюм з фініками, зверху - решту
рису. Накрийти все покришкою і тушкувати на маленькому вогні 20 хвилин.
5. Підготуйте шафран: для посилення аромати його необхідно розмочити в
гарячій воді (приблизно 30 мл або 1/6 склянки) і залишити настоюватися на
15-20 хвилин.

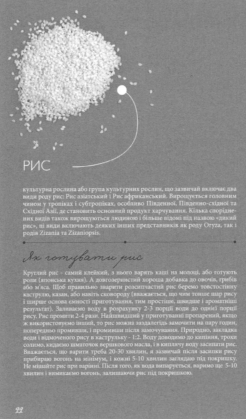

КУС-КУС

французькі рецепти

КУС-КУС
з зеленню та перцем

шпинат 60г

базилік 30г

перець 1 шт.

чорний перець 10г

кус-кус 400г

цибуля 1 шт.

1. У широкій пательні доводимо до кипіння бульйон, зменшуємо вогонь і кидаємо в нього морквину, нарізану кружальцями, і дрібно нарізану цибулю. Варимо 5-8 хвилин, до напівготовності моркви. Засипаємо кускус, розмішуємо, через 5 хвилин знімаємо з вогню. Покришку з пательні не знімаємо, — кускус повинен дійти.

2. Дрібно нарізаємо зелень, м'яту, цибулю та додаємо в кус-кус. Після цього додаємо помідори, огірки, перець, ізюм, шпинат. Перемішуємо.

3. Складаємо готовий кускус в миску, акуратно перемішуємо з помідорами і зеленню. Додаємо сир. Посипаємо пармезаном.

КУС-КУС
з цукіні та помідорами

помідори 100г

цибуля 1 шт.

картопля 75г

паприка 10г

італійські трави 10г

цукіні 1 шт.

кус-кус 500г

1. Овочі почистити (цукіні залишити зі шкіркою) і порізати на 4 частини, гарбуз-великими шматками.На дно каструлі покласти м'ясо і приправи, залити водою, довести до кипіння, посолити, додати цибулю і залишити варитися на середньому вогню.

2. Тим часом насипаємо крупу кус-кус у велику салатницю, заливаємо водою так, щоб вона покрила крупу, залишаємо на 10-15 хвилин. Коли крупа збере воду і розбухне, розминаємо її руками, щоб не було грудок і перекладаємо в пароварку і ставимо на каструлю з бульйоном. Покришкою не закривати.

3. Після того, як крупа добре прогріється, і з неї піде пар — залишаємо її на вогні 10 хвилин. Потім знімаємо пароварку з кускусом (бульйон залишається на вогні), і висипаємо кускус на велику тарілку. Аккуратно перемішуємо кілька разів, не допускаючи утворення грудок. У цей час додаємо у бульйон овочі, які варяться найдовше (морква, капуста, ріпа).

4. Коли знімаємо кус-кус з вогню відразу ж додамо до нього чайну ложку солі, по 2 ложки оливкової і вершкового масла. Все змішуємо.

РИС

італійські рецепти

РИС

культурна рослина або група культурних рослин, що зазвичай включає два види роду рис: Рис азіатський і Рис африканський. Вирощується головним чином у тропіках і субтропіках, особливо Південної, Південно-східної та Східної Азії, де становить основний продукт харчування. Кілька споріднених видів також вирощуються людиною і більше відомі під назвою «дикий рис», ці види включають деяких інших представників як роду Oryza, так і родів Zizania та Zizaniopsis.

Як готувати рис

Круглий рис - самий клейкий, з нього варять каші на молоці, або готують роли (японська кухня). А довгозернистий хороша добавка до овочів, грибів або м'яса. Щоб правильно зварити розсипчастий рис беремо товстостінну каструлю, казан, або навіть сковороду (вважається, що чим тонше шар рису і ширше основа ємності приготування, тим простіше, швидше і ароматніші результат). Заливаємо воду в розрахунку 2-3 порції води на одній порції рису. Рис промити 2-4 рази. Найшвидший у приготуванні пропарений, якщо ж використовуємо інший, то рис можна заздалегідь замочити на пару годин, попередньо промивши, і промиши після замочування. Природно, закладка води і відмоченого рису в каструлю - 1:2. Воду доводимо до кипіння, трохи солимо, кидаємо шматочок вершкового масла, і в киплячу воду засипати рис. Вважається, що варити треба 20-30 хвилин, я зазвичай після засипки рису прибираю вогонь на мінімум, і кожні 5-10 хвилин заглядаю під покришку. Не мішайте рис при варінні. Після того, як вода випарується, варимо ще 5-10 хвилин і вимикаємо вогонь, залишаючи рис під покришкою.

м'ята 100г

помідори черрі 150г

чорний перець 5г

рис 400г

зелена цибуля 2 шт.

РІЗОТТО
з помідорами

1. Цибулю почистити, помити і дрібно нарізати. Викласти сковорідку з 2 столовими ложками рослинного масла і обсмажити до напівпрозорої. Додати ретельно промитий рис і обсмажувати протягом 2 хвилин на маленькому вогні.

2. Додати томатну пасту, перемішати і готувати ще 2-3 хвилини. Влити вино і поступово підливаючи гарячий бульйон, готувати постійно помішуючи, поки рис не вбере в себе всю рідину.

3. Додати дрібно нарізані помідори черрі і чебрець. Влити ще одну склянку бульйону і помішувати, поки рис вбере в себе бульйон. Продовжувати підливати бульйон протягом 25 хвилин.

4. В'ялені помідори дрібно нарізати і перекласти в рис. Перемішати і додати тертий сир. Добавити спеції і знову перемішати.

Розкласти в тарілки, посипати тертим сиром і подати на стіл.

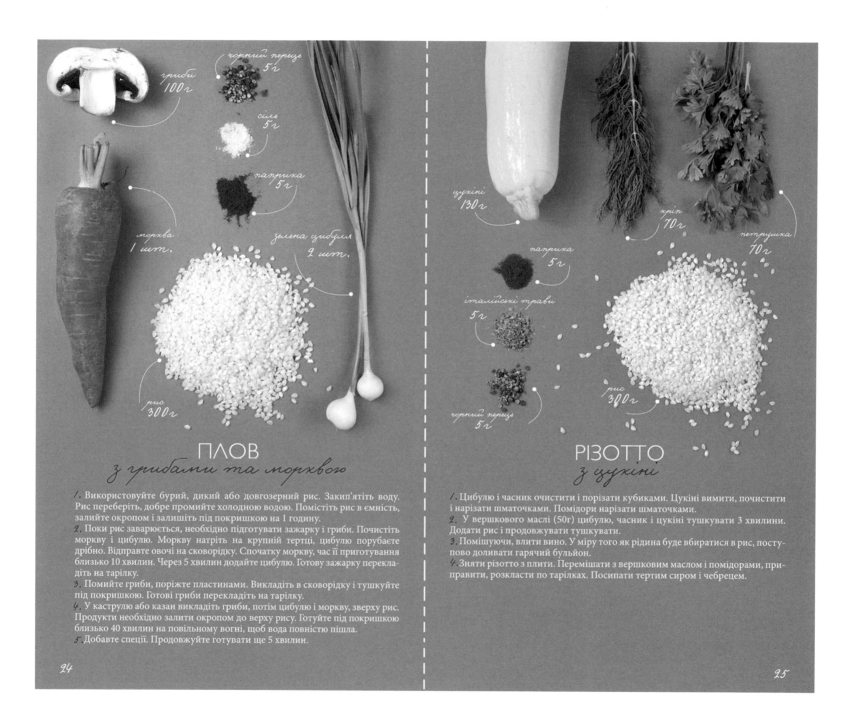

грибі
100 г

чорний перець
5 г

сіль
5 г

паприка
5 г

морква
1 шт.

зелена цибуля
2 шт.

рис
300 г

цукіні
130 г

хрін
70 г

петрушка
70 г

паприка
5 г

італійські трави
5 г

рис
300 г

чорний перець
5 г

ПЛОВ
з грибами та морквою

1. Використовуйте бурий, дикий або довгозерний рис. Закип'ятіть воду. Рис переберіть, добре промийте холодною водою. Помістіть рис в ємність, залийте окропом і залишіть під покришкою на 1 годину.
2. Поки рис заварюється, необхідно підготувати зажарку і гриби. Почистіть моркву і цибулю. Моркву натріть на крупній тертці, цибулю порубаєте дрібно. Відправте овочі на сковорідку. Спочатку моркву, час її приготування близько 10 хвилин. Через 5 хвилин додайте цибулю. Готову зажарку перекладіть на тарілку.
3. Помийте гриби, поріжте пластинами. Викладіть в сковорідку і тушкуйте під покришкою. Готові гриби перекладіть на тарілку.
4. У каструлю або казан викладіть гриби, потім цибулю і моркву, зверху рис. Продукти необхідно залити окропом до верху рису. Готуйте під покришкою близько 40 хвилин на повільному вогні, щоб вода повністю пішла.
5. Добавте спеції. Продовжуйте готувати ще 5 хвилин.

РІЗОТТО
з цукіні

1. Цибулю і часник очистити і порізати кубиками. Цукіні вимити, почистити і нарізати шматочками. Помідори нарізати шматочками.
2. У вершкового маслі (50г) цибулю, часник і цукіні тушкувати 3 хвилини. Додати рис і продовжувати тушкувати.
3. Помішуючи, влити вино. У міру того як рідина буде вбиратися в рис, поступово доливати гарячий бульйон.
4. Зняти різотто з плити. Перемішати з вершковим маслом і помідорами, приправити, розкласти по тарілках. Посипати тертим сиром і чебрецем.

Fame

- **Designer**
  Martina Casonato

- **Material**
  Jacket: 230gsm Fedrigoni Splendorgel;
  Text: 115gsm and 160gsm Fedrigoni Splendorgel

- **Size**
  170mm x 235mm

- **Photo Credit**
  Martina Casonato

Fame is the pilot issue of a self-initiated editorial project about food (fàme is Italian for hunger). Aimed at young cuisine amateurs, the volume is structured in eight sections, each of which explores a different aspect of food culture: from literature, cinema, music, and new technologies to interviews of young emerging chefs.

The final section is solely dedicated to a series of recipes (eight per month), and each issue focuses on eight seasonal ingredients. The recipes are specifically created to satisfy the needs of their young audience: healthy, affordable and achievable, and serving two people rather than the traditional four.

In order to achieve better legibility and immediacy, the designer uses a combination of pictograms and short instructions to easily guide readers through the recipes. Finally, a custom perforation on this back section allows readers to tear out their favorite recipes (which are purposefully printed on a thicker stock) to create their own personalized collection.

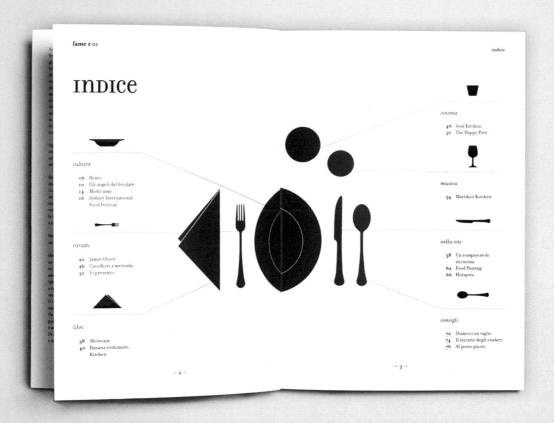

INDICE

MANGA GIAPPONESE (dei gloriosi tempi che furono). Scena tipo: l'eroina timida e impacciata porta al suo amato un pranzo da lei confezionato (comprensivo di pietanze simil-polipo) nella speranza di conquistare il suo cuore. *Quello è il bento.*

BENTO

Ovvero la fenomenologia di un semplice cestino da pranzo giapponese, per scoprire che poi, in fin dei conti, un semplice cestino da pranzo non è. La storia, i personaggi e i motivi che hanno reso il *bento* un vero e proprio simbolo della cultura alimentare orientale.

La cultura del cibo in Giappone assume delle connotazioni davvero affascinanti. Prendiamo l'esempio del *bento*, il tipico cestino da pranzo che tanto ha popolato nell'immaginario collettivo nipponico da diventare una vera e propria icona. Scopriremo che dietro il *bento* non si cela semplicemente del cibo da asporto, ma molto di più. Oggi un *bento* classico consiste per la metà di una porzione di riso, mentre per l'altra metà di contorni quali pesce, carne, verdure o uova. Queste ultime sono senza dubbio il contorno che va per la maggiore, sotto forma di *tamagoyaki* (omelette cucinate con sale e zucchero e tagliate a striscioline), oppure ancora fritte o strapazzate. Un'altro elemento ricorrente è la salsiccia, spesso tagliata in modo da assumere forme zoomorfe come quella della medusa. Non mancano poi carne fritta, pesce alla griglia, tortini e verdure (bollite, al vapore o sottaceto), ma il vero ingrediente chiave di ogni *bento* che si rispetti è la prugna. Non una prugna qualsiasi, bensì una varietà particolare chiamata *umeboshi* coltivata in Giappone e lasciata

133

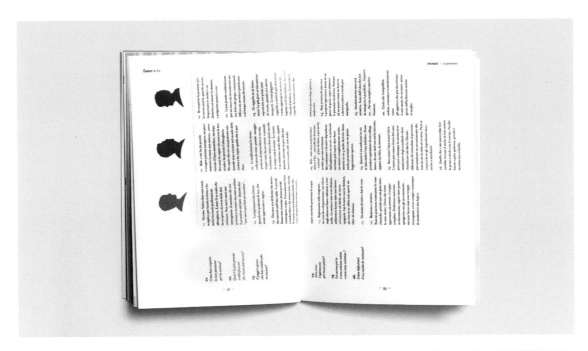

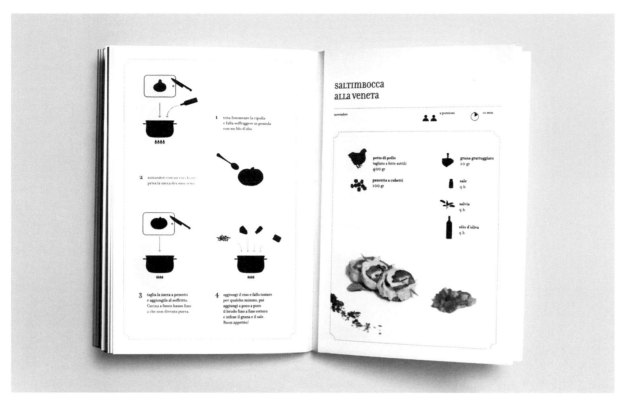

Cooking
with Colors

- **Designer**
  Juo-Yu Chang

- **Size**
  205mm x 275mm

- **Completion**
  2013

This is a book about Chinese cooking in harmony with nature; it has both aesthetic and practical functions. It introduces the Chinese way of keeping healthy—the Five-Color Theory—which suggests that people include five colors in every meal, because every color has its own nutritional value that is beneficial to different organs. The theory sorts all ingredients into the following colors: yellow, green, red, white, and black.

Color-coded recipes are included in one part of the book and the other part outlines the color theory. Recipes are accompanied by illustrations, which act as a universal language and help Western readers cross the cultural barrier and understand the concepts presented.

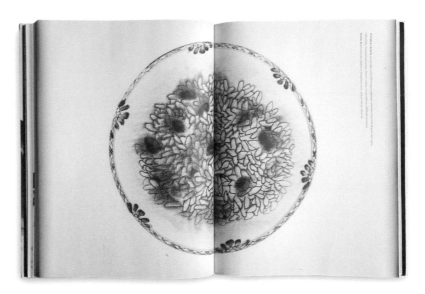

GRAPE AND BLACK TEA JELLY
Pu Tao Hong Cha Guo Dong

15 grape
½ apple
1 teabag black tea
2 tsp sugar
5 g gelatine
250 ml water
1 tsp rum
1 tsp lemon

Rinse the grape, and keep 6 grapes aside for late decoration. Remove the seeds from the other grape and shred them thinly.

Rinse apple, cut it into into cubes, set aside.

Boil a bowl of water and soak black teabag in water for 10 mins.

Add thinly shredded grapes, apple, sugar, rum in black tea, and cook it on a low heat for 5 mins. Add gelatine till it is dissolved.

Transfer grape mixture into containers, and put them in the refrigerator for 5 hrs. After the jelly is solid, cut 6 grapes in half and decorate them on top of the container.

BLACK

Seaweed, eggplant, shiitake mushrooms, black beans, black rice, black sesame seeds, kelp, and blue berries comprise the color category of black. This kind of food are rich in vitamin, trace elements, high quality of vegetable protein. It also contains antioxidants that help the immune system, prevent cancers and relieve allergies, respiratory problems.

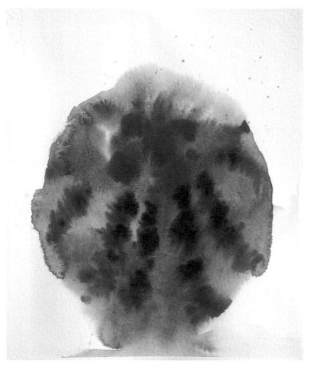

SUITABLE CHOICES are also key questions, male and female. If certain is known to relieve damp coldness such as dryness and excessive. In general, disorders of mucus from the lungs, bronchi and throat, coming from food culture.

---

whole body and the physiological functions are normal. Something important to mention here is the definition of organs from both Chinese and Western perspectives. When it comes to the definition of organs, from a TCM point of view, it is different from Western medicine. Organs are not simply anatomical substances, but more importantly represent the generalization of the physiology and pathology of certain systems of human body. For example, the heart in Western medicine means heart itself and its circulatory system, while in TCM, it includes not only the heart and circulatory system but also the central nervous system (a combination of brain and spine cord). In general, the meaning of organs in TCM is broader than just the organs themselves. It covers the interdependent relationships between them.

COOKING WITH FIVE COLORS

Five-color theory is used in Chinese cooking philosophy. It encourages people have five colors in every meal. Base on this principle to cook, nutrients naturally come into balance without doing complicated dietary calculations. Therefore, the cookbook is ordered by type of dish, so that reader can pick their preferable color from different type of dishes, and combine various-color spectrum. Through cooking with colors, people manage to achieve health.

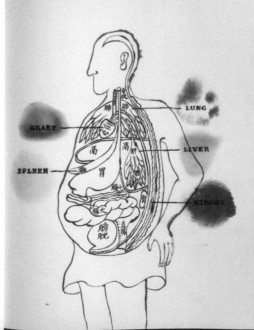

LUNG

HEART

LIVER

SPLEEN

KIDNEY

Cans' Combat

- **Designer**
  Carolin Lahmeyer

- **Material**
  Paper, Carton, Linen, Staple

- **Printing Technology**
  Embossing

- **Size**
  220mm x 300mm

- **Completion**
  2012

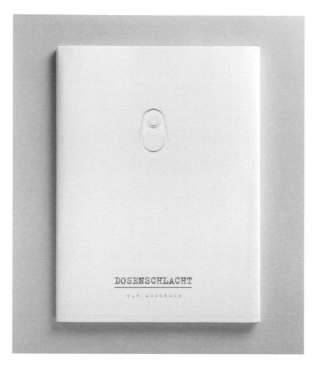

DOSENSCHLACHT

ein kochbuch

The creative cookbook 'Cans' Combat' (*Dosenschlacht*) brings together two passions of designer Carolin Lahmeyer—photography and cooking. It has a straightforward message: put the can opener aside and work with beautiful, fresh, healthy ingredients. With a little effort, you can still prepare a great meal quickly. Readers have the option of tearing perforated and stitched together 'take-out recipes' from the book to either take grocery shopping or share with friends— these provide a rich, tactile user experience.

The intriguing styling and food photography presents fresh vegetables in old cans or typical fast-food packaging that's been painted white. Set against a white background, the packaging has a uniform look and loses its previous identity, which, combined with the fresh produce, introduces elements of surprise and irony. The layout is simple, linked to scanned paper structures in the background.

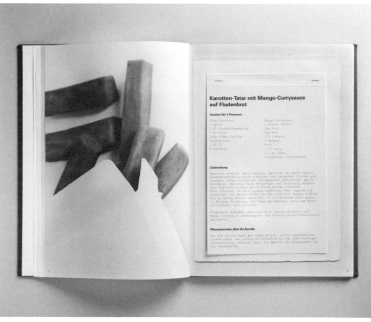

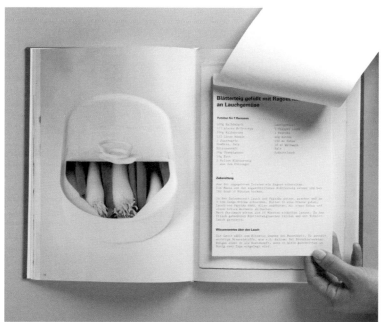

This cookbook about how to make sandwiches is also a toy! The cookbook component contains illustrated cooking tutorials explaining how to make 10 sandwiches, each on a separate spread. In the middle of each spread there is a plate showing how a slice of bread can become a delicious work of art.

Also an amusing toy for a child, the book is designed to be touched, transformed and played with. Its packaging is made up of cases that have the shape of a glove in them so that a child can stick their hand inside. A transparent envelope on the cover is invitingly tactile, made of several types of paper, a fabric patch, buttons, and rubber bands.

Cooking Game

- **Designer**
  Elena Gerasimova

- **Binding**
  Accordion Folding

- **Material**
  Coated Paper, Paperboard,
  Fabric, Buttons

- **Size**
  82mm x 108mm

- **Completion**
  2012

поросёнок

Ингредиенты:
1 котлета по-киевски
4 черные маслины без косточки
1 горошина
1 кружочек моркови
1 веточка базилика
1 стебелек укропа

Подготовка
Взять за основу котлеты по-киевски.

1 Уложить котлету на тарелку. Это «туловище» поросенка.
Надрезать горошину, оставив неразрезанной кожицу. Развернуть половинки горошины. Это «глаза». «Зрачки» вырезать из тонко срезанной кожуры черной маслины.
Уложить «глаза» на «поросенка».

2 В кружочке моркови вырезать два отверстия. Это «пятачок».
Уложить «пятачок» под «глаза».

3 Отрезать от базилика веточку с двумя листиками. Это «ушки».
Две черные маслины без косточки разрезать вдоль на половинки. Вырезать из каждой половинки небольшие треугольнички. Это

4 Из стебелька укропа сделать хвостик. Накрутить его по спирали вокруг зубочистки, слегка прижать, чтобы он сохранил форму.

4 Уложить на «поросенка» «хвостик» и «ушки», приставить «копыта».

3

4

5

градусник

Ингредиенты:
1. огурец
кусочек красного сладкого перца
кусочек желтого сладкого перца
1 ломтик плавленого сыра для тостов
веточка базилика
лист зеленого салата
сливочное масло или майонез

Подготовка
Взять за основу котлету по-киевски.

1 Огурец разрезать вдоль и отрезать от него тонкий ломтик.
Вырезать из кусочка красного сладкого перца кружочек и полосочку. Из желтого перца вырезать полосочку такой же ширины. Это «столбик термометра».

2 Срезать с них лишнюю мякоть.
Уложить на ломтик огурца «столбик термометра».

3 Ломтик тостерного хлеба намазать сливочным маслом или майонезом, сверху положить ломтик плавленого сыра для тостов, уложить «термометр».

3 Стебель базилика нарезать на отрезки равной длины.
Выложить их в виде шкалы (делений) термометра.

4 Уложить бутерброд на лист зеленого салата.

3

4

5

олень

Ингредиенты:
1 вареная морковь
1 лист зеленого салата
2 кружочка репчатого лука
2 черная маслина
1 огурец
1 горошина
2 мелкоплодных помидора
кетчуп

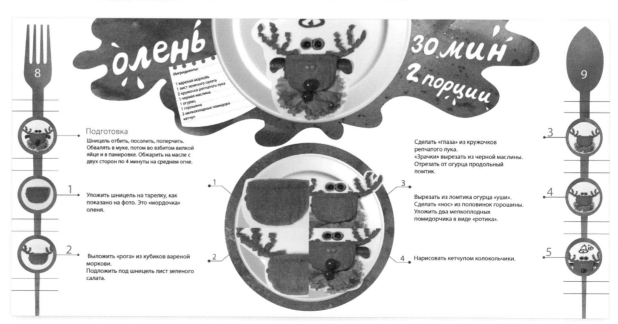

Подготовка
Шницель отбить, посолить, поперчить. Обвалять в муке, потом во взбитом вилкой яйце и в панировке. Обжарить на масле с двух сторон по 4 минуты на среднем огне.

1 Уложить шницель на тарелку, как показано на фото. Это «мордочка» оленя.

2 Выложить «рога» из кубиков вареной моркови.
Подложить под шницель лист зеленого салата.

3 Сделать «глаза» из кружочков репчатого лука.
«Зрачки» вырезать из черной маслины.
Отрезать от огурца продольный ломтик.

3 Вырезать из ломтика огурца «уши». Сделать «нос» из половинок горошины.
Уложить два мелкоплодных помидорчика в виде «ротика».

4 Нарисовать кетчупом колокольчики.

3

4

5

Maryanne Shearer is the author of this book based on the global tea brand T2. The goal was to produce an exciting book about tea, and the typography was to be in keeping with the design features of the T2 company.

This project was a designer's dream, as every page required a new layout or a new way to display the visual material, using different storytelling methods throughout. The major design challenge was how to inject wit into serious subjects such as tea history and tea processing. This was solved by using tea leaves as visual elements, generously incorporating them into illustrative components and infographics.

The cover features an illustration of the iconic 'Barry' teapot from T2, with steam designed from tea leaves coming out of its spout. Embossing was used effectively on the teapot, logo and some of the tea leaves, giving the book an unexpected tactility. The top of the lid and spout of the teapot are embellished with gold leaf foil, providing a lift from the heavy black and orange of the rest of the cover and adding a touch of brilliance. The edges of the pages are sprayed with orange, providing the finishing touch to this 'book as an object' challenge.

T2—
The Book

- Designer
  Evi O.

- Material
  Uncoated Endpapers,
  Head and Tail Band

- Printing Technology
  Non-Scuff Lamination,
  Embossing, Gold Foil

- Size
  250mm x 195mm

- Completion
  2015

- Photo Credit
  Magenta Burgin

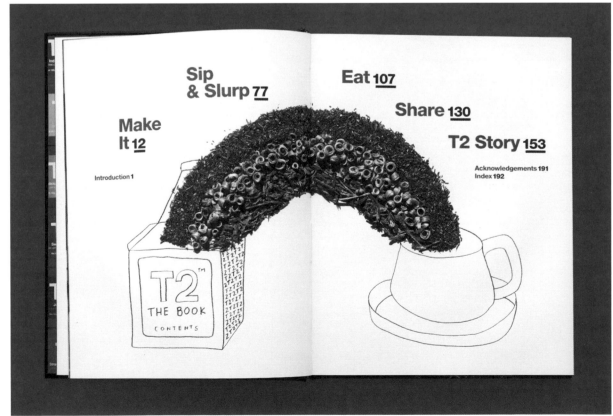

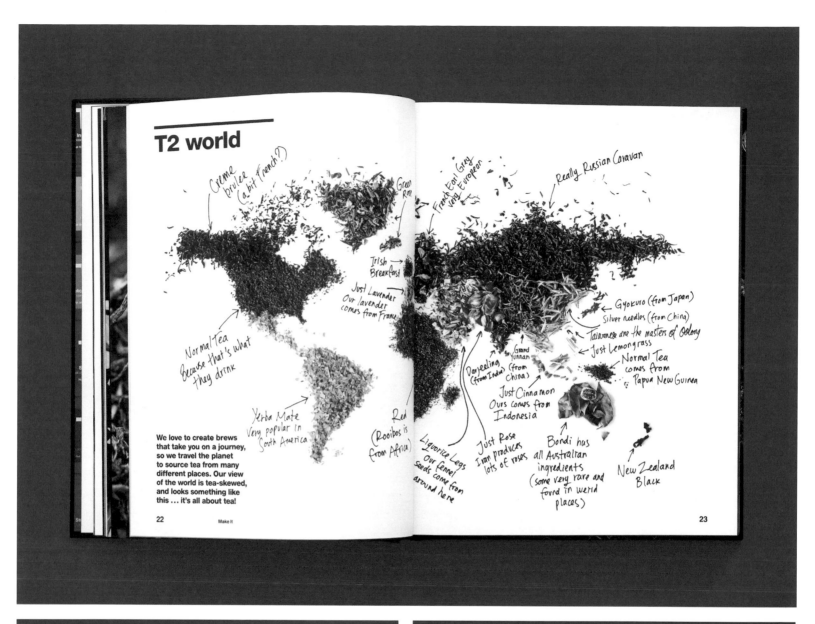

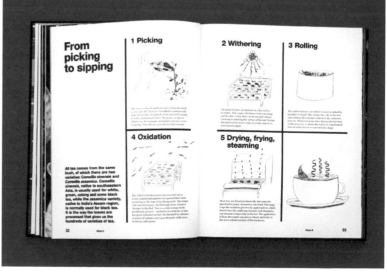

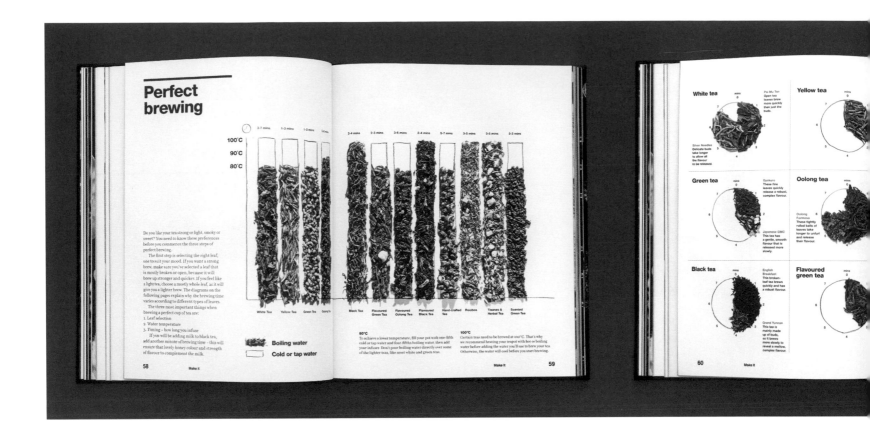

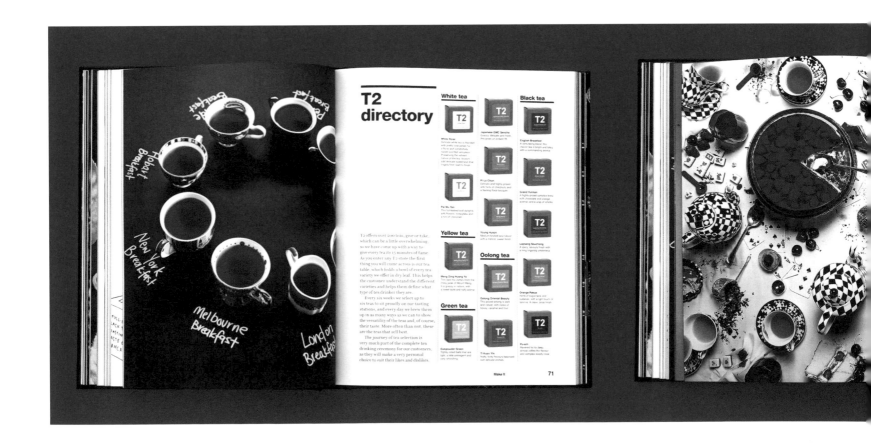

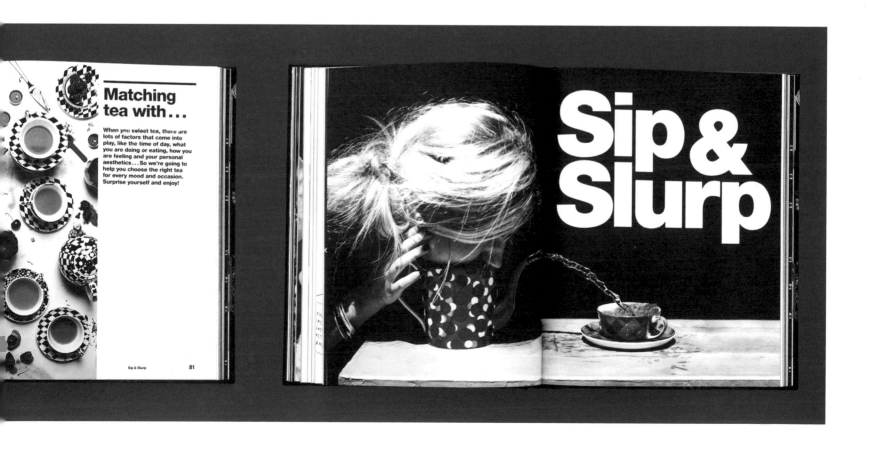

GIZ
Cookbook

- **Design Agency**
  Backbone Branding

- **Designers**
  Stepan Azaryan,
  Karen Gevorgyan,
  Arabo Sargsyan,
  Armenak Grigoryan,
  Anahit Margaryan

- **Material**
  Paper, Carton, Wood

- **Size**
  230mm x 230mm

- **Completion**
  2013

- **Photo Credit**
  Backbone Branding,
  Suren Manvelyan

The purpose of creating this cookbook was to preserve Armenian culinary recipes. An Armenian grandmother–botanist character was created for the purposes of the book, and this grandmother shares her cooking secrets 'from meadows to kitchen.' This fictional character devoted her whole life to investigating the wild herbs of Armenia and generously passes on her rich experience to future generations in this book, a collection of wild herb recipes.

The overall design of the book gives the impression that it's a handwritten diary kept by the grandmother, which effectively draws readers in. There's even a wooden spoon—a gift from the grandmother—attached to the cover!

George Calombaris is a celebrity chef from a Greek family. The aim of this book was to showcase his passion for Greek food and his never-ending energy, as well as to incorporate his love of street art into the pages.

Earl Carter's photography combined with Lee Blaylock's styling brought a playful and inventive approach to the food photography, showing the food in a relaxed way, as if it was about to be eaten.

The design direction harmoniously juxtaposes the moody photography with bright colors, hand-done typography, and a series of cartoon illustrations. Each recipe page features different graffiti marks, and often a recipe runs over four pages, showcasing shots of the cooking process and beautiful still lifes of key ingredients.

The endpapers feature an illustration of a table full of empty dishes and include a sticker sheet containing more illustrations of some of the key dishes and ingredients in the book—this was included so readers could create their own feast on the 'empty table' endpapers, adding a level of interaction with the book. The graphic cover features typography influenced by street art and an illustrated lemon, an iconic ingredient in Greek cuisine.

Greek

- **Designer**
  Evi O.

- **Material**
  Uncoated Endpapers,
  Custom Sticker Sheet,
  Linen Ribbon,
  Head and Tail Band

- **Printing Technology**
  PLC with Non-Scuff
  Lamination, Debossing

- **Size**
  205mm x 270mm

- **Completion**
  2015

- **Photo Credit**
  Earl Carter

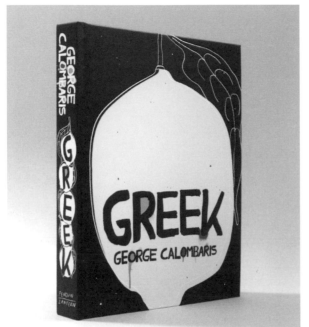

Contents

MY MUM'S CHICKEN NUGGETS

– WHERE ALL IS NOT AS IT SEEMS

As an Aussie Greek boy growing up in an ethnic family all I wanted was to be like my next-door neighbours. I wanted to dress like them, act like them and have my mum cook food like them. One of the dishes I most wanted Mum to make was chicken nuggets. Yep, chicken nuggets. So Mum said no problem and busied herself in the kitchen. For years we loved our mum's chicken nuggets until one day we discovered that they were in fact lamb brains! Crispy and crunchy on the outside and beautifully creamy on the inside. At first I was outraged, but in the end I was grateful that my mother cooks with whole and real food. I can't wait for my kids to ask me to cook them chicken nuggets!

We should all be eating this forgotten meat. Brains are super healthy and, when cooked well, they're absolutely delicious. I love to serve them with a little tartare sauce or sometimes just a squeeze of lemon juice. Make sure you soak them overnight in water first to clean them thoroughly.

I'm a firm believer that we must eat from nose to tail. The animal has been sacrificed for us and we must respect it as chefs and customers by using every bit. We waste far too much food in Australia. My mum taught us this valuable lesson as we were growing up – she always found a way to make things last and never threw anything out. It's so simple really. I guess when you have had struggles in your life (like my mum) you don't take anything for granted. Respect your friends, respect your food and where it came from and, above all, don't take anything for granted.

Little Brunch Book

- **Designer**
  Alejandra García Pérez

- **Material**
  Uncoated Paper, Cardboard

- **Size**
  150mm x 200mm

- **Completion**
  2015

The *Little Brunch Book* is intended as a monthly publication that's available by subscription. Each issue focuses on a different country and contains three different brunch or breakfast recipes and their history, notes on their preparation, and interviews with the recipe creators. The blue and off-white colors used in the design of this first issue about Mexico are meant to reflect Mexican tableware.

Its clever concertina-fold design means that the book can be spread out and viewed all at once, making it easier for the reader to follow the recipes as they don't have to keep going back and forth through the book.

Since the recipes and breakfast/country themes are predominant, the typographical elements used are simple and work to support the design. Gotham is the main typeface for the titles, and its size varies to create a hierarchy between the recipe names and the different sections. To contrast with this sans-serif font, Garamond is used for the main text (size 8 point).

The leading is slightly loose so that the reader can follow the recipe without getting lost; this also gives the design a more relaxed feel, which goes nicely with the breakfast theme. Generous amounts of white space create balance between the evenly spread text, graphic elements and illustrations.

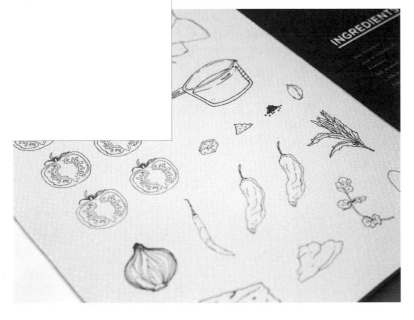

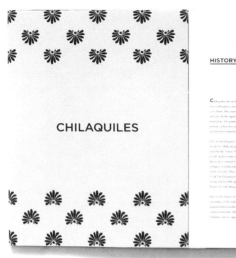

CHILAQUILES

HISTORY

Chilaquiles are, at their most basic form, a collection of tortilla pieces, usually fried, with a chili sauce poured over them. The exact food's origin began to surface and after all the liquid of whatever sauce they are immersed in. The point time to eat chilaquiles is between cooking, when they are no longer crunchy but have not yet turned completely soft.

The word chilaquiles comes from the ancient Nahuatl word for "chilis and greens." The Nahuatl language was used by the Aztecs. It originated in Central Mexico and is still spoken today in select communities. Chilaquiles are a firmly rooted food in many Mexican families, owing to a traditional legacy that has rooted for hundreds of years. They came to America via "The Spanish Cook" by Encarnación Pinedo in 1898. However, this recipe did not fully appreciate or replicate the simple beauty of real chilaquiles.

Part of the beauty of chilaquiles lies in the incredibly versatility of the dish. Though the basic ingredients only required few a tortillas and a chili sauce, nearly every variation includes additional ingredients and garnishes. Chicken, onions, eggs, queso fresco and other additions

are found in many chilaquiles recipes. Chilaquiles were made as a base, which could be added to as ingredients became available. Often these ingredients were identifying markers of a particular region or family.

Chilaquiles are created using ingredients that are widely available, and cheap. Their function often has been to extend the use of expensive portions in dishes. Small pieces of meat, cheese, or eggs could be added to a plate of chilaquiles, providing a large amount of calories while only using a fraction of the expensive ingredients. This dish was created as a budget conscious staple, and now it has become a home cooked classic.

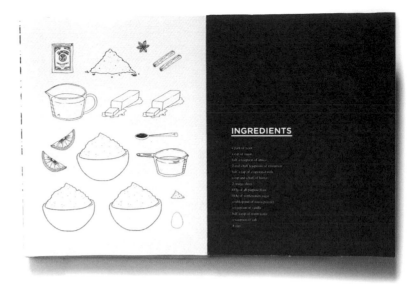

INGREDIENTS

a pinch of yeast
a cup of sugar
half a teaspoon of anise
2 and a half teaspoons of cinnamon
half a cup of evaporated milk
a cup and a half of butter
2 orange slices
400g of all purpose flour
110g of confectioners sugar
a tablespoon of cocoa powder
a teaspoon of vanilla
half a cup of warm water
a teaspoon of salt
4 eggs

RECIPE

Totopos

Red salsa

Preparing

Decoration

Servings: 2
Cooking time: 30 minutes

CHAMPURRADO

HISTORY

Many people know the history of chocolate, how the Spanards discovered the Mayans using it. They though it was a superfood. The Mayans made a drink from what I have read the first drink consisted of roasted cocoa beans, chiles, vanilla, cinnamon, almonds and hazelnuts all ground and mixed with water and cooked.

It still does give resistance and strength to the people that work the land of the cocoa plantations in the Southern part of México. While working as a School Teacher for 2 years in a Cacao Bean plantation in Tabasco, I saw first hand how the men would go to work very early in the morning, carrying with them a full canteen of "pozol." A drink made of water, corn dough, and ground cocoa beans. Pozol sustained them in their hard work until the midday hour when the high temperatures would reach 90 degrees in the jungle like area of southeast Mexico.

The chocolate used for the Mexican version of hot cocoa is different that the mixes we use here. It is sold in cakes, round tablets as seen in the picture above. Here are two popular brands, Ibarra and Abuelita. This is bittersweet chocolate ground with cinnamon and piloncillo (unrefined sugar) the sugar isn't dissolved so it has a different consistency that chocolate we are used to. My personal favorite brand is Mayordomo, not commonly found here but very good, along with the above ingredients it has ground almonds. It is the rectangular box seen in the picture below.

Champurrado is a chocolate-based atole, a warm and thick Mexican drink, prepared with either masa de maíz (lime-treated-corn dough), masa harina (a dried version of this dough), or corn flour (simply very finely ground dried corn, especially local varieties grown for atole); panela, water or milk; and occasionally containing cinnamon, anise seed and or vanilla.

Champurrado is traditionally served with churros in the morning as a simple breakfast or as a late afternoon snack. Champurrado is also very popular during Día de Muertos (Day of the Dead in Spanish) and at Las Posadas (the Christmas Season) where it is served alongside tamales. Champurrado may also be made with alcohol.

CONCHAS

The concha is a slightly sweet roll with a shell patterned topping made from the traditional sugar crust
paste (pasta) – a mixture of white flour, sugar and
butter, sometimes added with cinnamon or chocolate.

Conchas are named after the shape of their sugar
topping, which resembles a seashell. Conchas do have a
hardened crust, but it is sugary, thick, crispy and crumbles right after it in your mouth as you take a bite. Right after
you break through that crust, there is a fluffy, soft, sweet
roll made with flour, butter, yeast and eggs. With such
a pleasing experience, no wonder it is one of Mexico's
most famous sweet rolls or pan dulce.

Pan Dulce translates to "Sweet Bread" in English and
it was an indigenous food in Mexico. Wheat was intro-
duced in Mexico by the Spanish during the time of the
conquest. It was a religious necessity because it is the
only grain deemed acceptable by the Catholic Church
for making communion wafers. The first bakeries in
Mexico started in the 1520s and were not very popular.
They only sought to supply the Indigenous people how
to bake and as the Spanish and Mexican population grew
so did the popularity of bread.

HISTORY

The consumption of bread became a staple in Mexico,
especially as a breakfast meal with hot chocolate. By
the end of the 17th century there were hundreds of
bakeries in Mexico and varieties were differentiated by
social class, white breads, also know as pan floreado,
were reserved for the nobility and rich. The lower
class ate "Pambazo," made with darker flour. French
influence on Mexican baking also started in the colonial
period, leading one staple bread still found today, the
bolillo (similar to a crusty French roll). Although the
earliest breads were the most basic, bakeries specializing
in sweet breads, called bizcocherías in Mexico, are noted
as early as 1554, and are well-established by the end of
the 17th century.

By the end of the 18th century, most bakeries had people dedicated to sweet breads. The creative contribution
of French baked goods to Mexico's cuisine peaked in
the early 19th Century during the dictatorship of Por-
firio Díaz. Skilled Mexican bakers adopted French techniques to create new bread designs with colorful names.
Today, Mexican bakers are among the most inventive in
the world, it is estimated that there are between 500 and
2,000 types of breads currently produced in Mexico.

INGREDIENTS

a tablespoon of vanilla
a bar of dark chocolate
half a cup of cornstarch
a cinnamon stick
half a cup of brown sugar
4 cups of milk

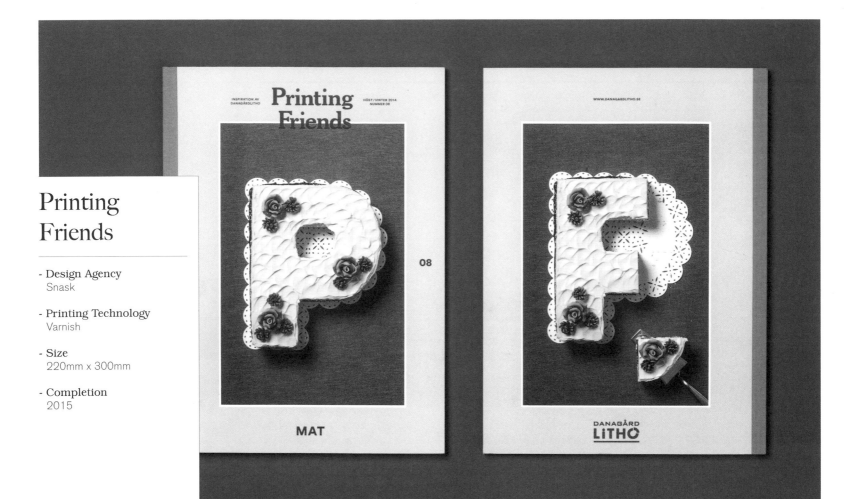

Printing Friends

- **Design Agency**
  Snask

- **Printing Technology**
  Varnish

- **Size**
  220mm x 300mm

- **Completion**
  2015

Printing Friends is an influential and exclusive print magazine about design and creativity published in Sweden. Each issue focuses on a particular theme—in this case, food—and is presented in an accessible and down-to-earth way. Different creators are showcased in each issue in order to inspire the creative industry; their personal stories are enhanced by illustrations, photography and typography.

In this issue, *Printing Friends* took a culinary trip around the world and ate mashed potato typography, a coconut flavored 'space burger,' and a knitted hot dog, among many other delicacies.

09

VEM:	BOR:
David Schwen	Minneapolis
YRKE:	WEB:
Art director &	Dschwen.com
Illustratör	

David Schwen kommer från reklambranschen och driver idag designstudion Dschwen i Minneapolis. Under de senaste åren har han gjort branding-, design- och illustrationsprojekt för kunder som Skittles, Urban Outfitters och Penguin Books.

The Matchmaker

DET FINNS EN TYDLIG FLIRT MED POPULÄRKULTUR I DET SOM DESIGNERN DAVID SCHWEN GÖR. KANSKE ÄR DET DÄRFÖR HAN UNDER DE SENASTE ÅREN FÅTT ETT STORT FÖLJANDE I SOCIALA MEDIER. PÅ INSTAGRAM BJUDER HAN SINA 93 000 FÖLJARE PÅ LEKFULLA STOP MOTION-FILMER OCH FÄRGGLADA STILLEBEN FRÅN HANS VARDAG. ETT AV HANS MEST DELADE PROJEKT ÄR FOOD ART PAIRINGS.

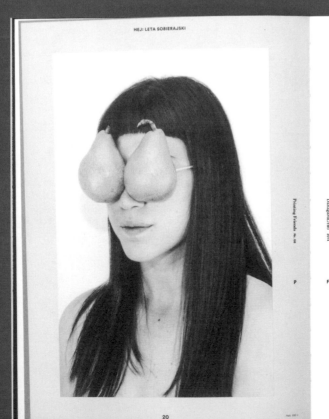

VEM:	BOR:
Leta Sobierajski	New York
YRKE:	WEB:
Art Director	letasobierajski.net

Google, Nylon Magazine och IBM är bara några som samarbetat med Leta Sobierajski under de senaste åren. I hennes dagliga jobb rör hon sig obehindrat mellan grafisk design, foto, konst och styling. Hennes stil kännetecknas ofta av udda stilleben för print, digitalt och rörligt.

LETA SOBIERAJSKI
Add/Ends
03:

LETA SOBIERAJSKI HITTAR DET FINA I VARDAGLIGA OBJEKT SOM TEJPRULLAR, OKOKTA ÄGG OCH TANDPETARE. FÖR PRINTING FRIENDS BERÄTTAR HON OM VARFÖR HON BÖRJAR RÖRA SIG BORT FRÅN ATT JOBBA MED FRUKT SOM BLIVIT HENNES SIGNUM OCH OM HUR EN TOAPAPPERSRULLE LADE GRUNDEN FÖR HELA HENNES KREATIVITET.

MAT: REVERSED VOLUMES

80

Reversed

MISCHER' TRAXLER

Volumes

VEM: Katharina Mischer & Thomas Traxler YRKE: Designers
BOR: Wien WEB: mischertraxler.com

Vi blev till slut intresserade av den negativa ytan mellan frukten och den existerande skålen själv — vi tänkte att frukten på något sätt formade luften mellan.

"En dag när jag la *två olika Pantonefärger* bredvid varandra kom jag att tänka på hur människor *parar ihop olika matvaror med* Efter det gjo *Food Art Pai* i sociala me

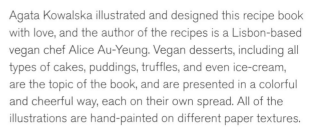

Agata Kowalska illustrated and designed this recipe book with love, and the author of the recipes is a Lisbon-based vegan chef Alice Au-Yeung. Vegan desserts, including all types of cakes, puddings, truffles, and even ice-cream, are the topic of the book, and are presented in a colorful and cheerful way, each on their own spread. All of the illustrations are hand-painted on different paper textures.

Ingredients are listed on the left-hand pages. Pages on the right-hand side unfold to reveal infographics that step the reader through the preparation of each dessert; combined with the ingredients page, these flaps make it easy for readers to follow the recipe. The infographics are drawn as though they're on a blackboard, giving the impression that the instructions are being explained by a teacher in a cooking class. Other illustrations show roughly cut pieces of cake or crumbs on a tablecloth, lending a handmade feel to the book.

The hardcover is a three-dimensional illustration of a café exterior. An awning-like flap was included on the cover not only for decoration, but also to function as a stand, further enhancing the book's usability.

Sweets

- **Designer**
  Agata Kowalska

- **Material**
  Maple White RJ Paper

- **Size**
  220mm x 220mm

- **Completion**
  2014

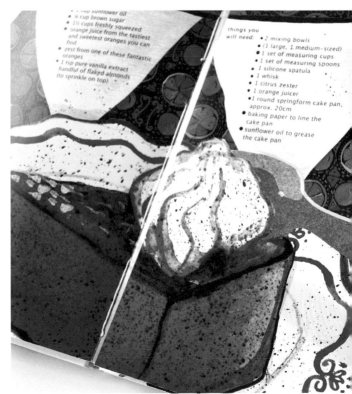

The Designers' Cookbook

- **Designer**
  Laura Dale Williams

- **Binding**
  Envelope Style Folding

- **Material**
  White Paper, Purple Paper

- **Size**
  70mm x 70mm

- **Completion**
  2012

- **Photo Credit**
  John Ord

Having a particular interest in print design and handmade books, designer Laura Dale Williams began *The Designers' Cookbook* by experimenting with different and unusual binding techniques. Once Williams decided on the structure of the book, she began thinking about the content. She wanted the recipes to represent a variety of visual principles used by graphic designers. Five recipes were chosen: 'Traditional Design' is represented by a roast dinner; 'Experimental Design' by a peach, goat's cheese and balsamic pizza; 'Collaborative Design' by fairy cakes; 'Simple Design' by beans on toast; and 'Precise Design' by sushi.

Each recipe is laid out on a single sheet of paper that folds around a concertina spine. Careful attention was given to the layout of each sheet to ensure all elements lined up when folded around the spine. To view each recipe, users pull out individual sheets and unfold them. Once each page is fully expanded, the simple and clean layout is revealed, showing a list of ingredients and clear cooking instructions, along with photographs of the raw ingredients and final dish.

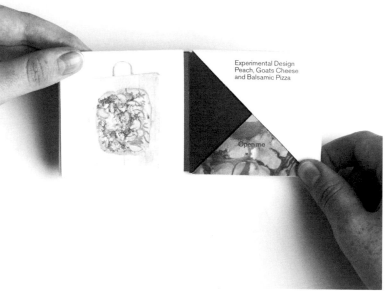

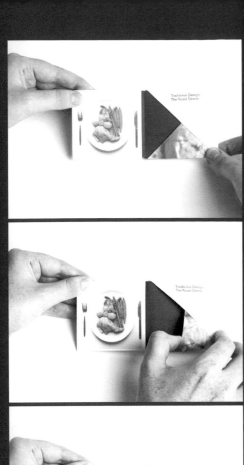

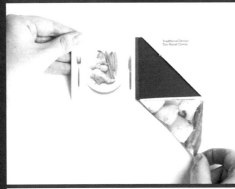
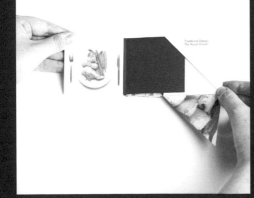

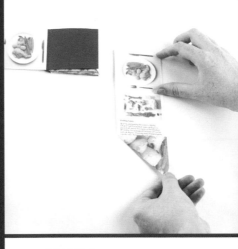

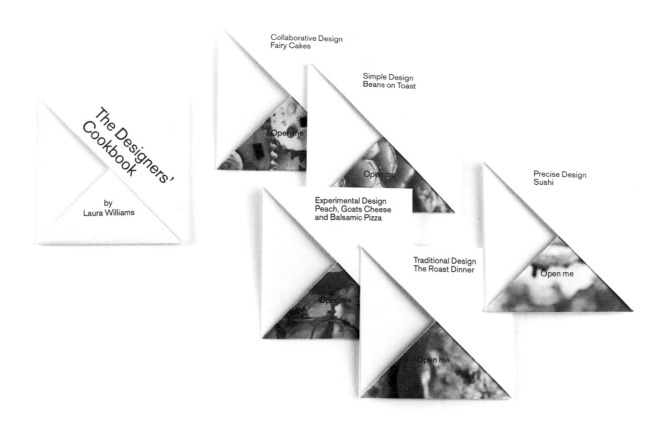

Collaborative Design
Fairy Cakes

Simple Design
Beans on Toast

The Designers'
Cookbook

by
Laura Williams

Precise Design
Sushi

Experimental Design
Peach, Goats Cheese
and Balsamic Pizza

Traditional Design
The Roast Dinner

Open me

Open me

Open me

Open me

Open me

Instructions

Preheat the oven at 180°C.
Start by beating the butter and the sugar
together until fluffy. Add the eggs and mix
well before folding in the flour. Stir until

Instructions

Slice the bread into slices. Place Slices of
Bread into the toaster and toast until brown.

Whilst the bread is toasting, empty the beans
into a pan and bring to a boil. When the toast
is ready, place onto plate and lightly butter.

Instructions

Preheat the oven at 190°C.
Combine flour, salt, sugar, and yeast in a
large bowl. Mix in oil and warm water.

Spread out on a large pizza pan suitable for
the oven by moulding the pizza base into

Instructions

Boil the rice in a large sauce pan for
25 minutes. Drain and allow to cool fully.

Place a s

Instructions

Start by preheating the oven to 20
Chop in half the peeled onion
place both inside the
Smother the
and rub

The Designers'
Cookbook

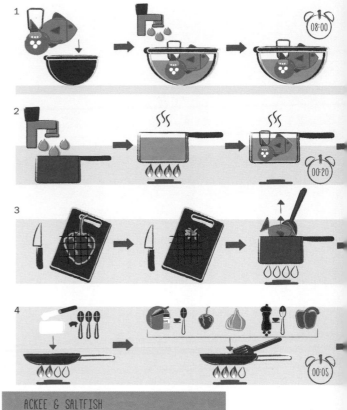

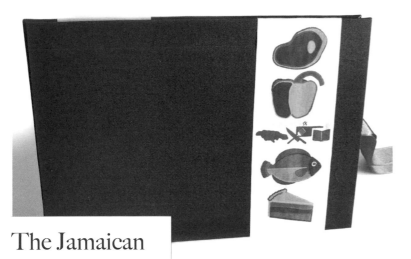

The Jamaican Cookbook

- **Designer**
  Chloe Ainsley

- **Material**
  Jacket: Gemini Olympic Millboard;
  Text: 135gsm China White Colorplan Paper, 135gsm Stone Colorplan Paper

- **Size**
  210mm x 297mm

- **Completion**
  2013

ACKEE & SALTFISH

The Jamaican Cookbook is a predominantly nonverbal and eye-opening exploration into Jamaican cuisine targeted at young adults. Its aim is to raise the profile of traditional Jamaican recipes while also addressing, in a non-authoritative way, current concerns over people's distorted knowledge of nutrition and food preparation.

Twenty recipes are included in this handmade cookbook with hardback cover. The pages are bound together with a concertina fold spine, which allows the book to open like a conventional book and also the pages to be pulled out in a line so that key information can be easily compared across the recipe collection.

Recipes have been constructed using a lively, vibrant pictographic system of symbols, which appear either in isolation or in various combinations. Each recipe takes the viewer on a wordless journey of discovery, decoding familiar and unfamiliar foods and flavors.

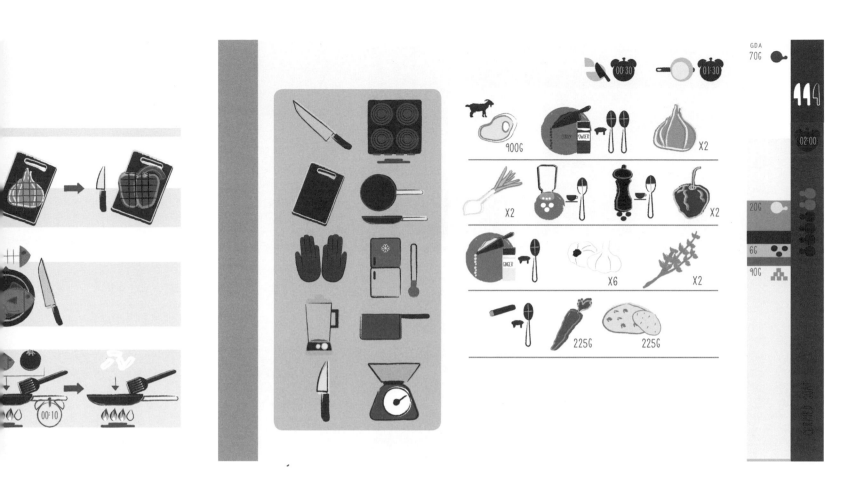

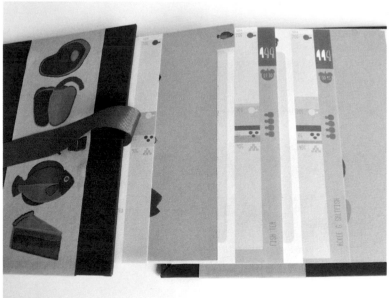

The People's Supermarket Cookbook

- **Designers**
  Kate McPartland,
  Radek Husak

- **Material**
  100 percent Recycled
  Unbleached Stock

- **Size**
  148mm x 210mm

- **Completion**
  2013

This cookbook reflects the diversity and warmth of London-based, nonprofit supermarket The People's Supermarket and its community. The aim was to design an accessible cookbook, full of personality, that would complement the supermarket's existing branding and communicate its ethos. The book contains stories and memories of community members' favorite foods, along with 60 recipes. It is an optimistic cookbook for everyday cooking.

Its A5 size was guided by a storybook format; because it is light and compact, readers can easily flick through it or read the content in its entirety. A handwritten font is used for titles and quotes and a characterful serif font for body text, which gives the book typographic interest and variety. The designers, Kate McPartland and Radek Husak, created a series of lively and colorful collages, with hints of old British eccentricity, to bring the recipes to life.

The Enjoyment
of Rice

- **Designer**
  Jessie Ning

- **Material**
  148gsm Proline Uncoated Paper

- **Size**
  180mm x 180mm

- **Photo Credit**
  Jessie Ning

Jessie Ning's obsession with rice—the most mundane yet exquisite grain, which can be said to represent life— was the inspiration for this book. White, glutinous, brown, and black rice are some of the categories covered in *The Enjoyment of Rice*. These are only a few members of the rice family, the diversity of which is difficult to encompass in one book.

Ning's original photographs are included in the design and rice paper was used as a background for the images. The typography choices of serif fonts (Bodoni and Bembo) highlight the elegant and traditional aspects of rice. Layouts are crafted and refined, with great attention to detail and with a consistent aesthetic, from the recipes and photography to the typography treatments. From planning to preparation, photo shoots and layouts, the process of making this book was very involved.

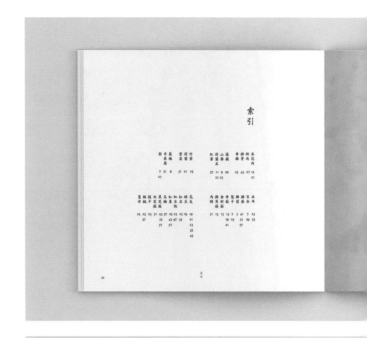

糙米

MILLET:
Red Bean Cube

1 Rinse the millet
2 Steam the millet with rose petals in the water 20 mins.
3 Shape the red bean paste into cubes and wrap them with the cooked millet, which has a rosy flavor.

WHITE RICE:
Snow Pea Porridge

1 Rinse and soak the rice in cold water 30 mins.
2 Add the rice to the boiling water
3 Heat on high; lower to gentle heat after 5 mins.
4 Stir after 20 min. Add the vegetable oil and salt
5 Let the porridge boil 1 hr.
6 Peel and scald snow peas
7 Mash and add snow peas to the porridge
8 Stir, and let sit 5 min

GLUTINOUS RICE:
Lakeside Glutinous Rice

1 Rinse and soak the rice in water with salt 4 hrs.
2 Wash and cut the lotus root into thick slices
3 Stuff the glutinous rice into the holes of the lotus root
4 Steam the stuffed lotus root with water and fresh lily bulbs 30 mins.
5 Make the syrup with: rock sugar, water, and tapioca flour
6 Coat the ready-to-serve dish with the syrup.

Black Rice

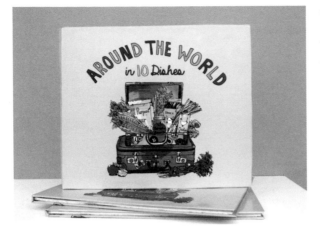

Children today often have the problem of 'food neophobia' or the fear of tasting new or unfamiliar foods. To help counter this, Sarah Park designed and illustrated this book to promote global cuisines and introduce children to exotic and authentic dishes from Europe all the way to Africa. The colorful and light illustrations are child-friendly, while the simple design aesthetic offers a fun and easy experience for both children and their parents. *Around the World in 10 Dishes* aims to help expand children's taste towards unfamiliar meals and challenge them to discover new ingredients.

Around the World in 10 Dishes

- **Designer**
  Sarah Park

- **Size**
  203mm x 254mm

- **Completion**
  2015

- **Photo Credit**
  Sarah Park

INDIAN Hand Pies

Ingredients:

- 1 TBSP GROUND CUMIN
- 1 SMALL ONION, MINCED
- 1 TSP CINNAMON
- 1 TBSP GRATED GINGER
- Chicken Stock
- ½ CUP FROZEN PEAS DEFROSTED
- 1 POTATO DICED INTO ¼ INCH CUBE
- PINCH OF SALT
- 2 GARLIC CLOVES MINCED
- ⅓ CUP CHICKEN BROTH
- ⅛ TSP CAYENNE PEPPER
- 1 TSP TURMERIC
- 2 TBSP MINCED PARSLEY
- 1 EGG BEATEN EGG WASH
- PEPPER
- 1 LB GROUND LAMB
- 2 TBSP MINCED CILANTRO
- 1 TBSP PAPRIKA
- 2 LBS OF PIZZA DOUGH

① SAUTÉ
IN A LARGE SKILLET OVER HIGH HEAT, SAUTÉ THE LAMB UNTIL NO LONGER PINK, ABOUT 8 MINUTES.

② ADD VEGGIES
POUR AWAY THE RENDERED FAT, THEN ADD THE CHICKEN BROTH, ALL THE SPICES, & THE ONION, POTATO, GARLIC, GINGER & HERBS. SIMMER UNTIL THE POTATO IS COOKED THROUGH, ABOUT 12 MINUTES.

③ STIR EVENLY
REMOVE THE SKILLET FROM THE HEAT & STIR IN THE PEAS. SPREAD THE MIX ON A BAKING SHEET & COOL FOR 20 MINUTES. STIR IN THE SEASONED EGG UNTIL EVENLY BLENDED.

④ FOLD + CRIMP
HEAT THE OVEN TO 375°. CUT THE PIZZA DOUGH INTO TWELVE 6-INCH ROUNDS. DIVIDE THE FILLING EVENLY AMONG THE DOUGH PORTIONS, MAKING A MOUND IN THE CENTER OF EACH ROUND. BRUSH THE EDGES WITH THE EGG WASH, THEN FOLD EACH PIE IN HALF & CRIMP ITS EDGES.

⑤ BRUSH
PLACE THE PIES ON A BAKING SHEET. BRUSH THE TOPS WITH THE REMAINING EGG WASH & MAKE A ½-INCH LONG SLIT IN THE TOP OF EACH ONE.

⑥ BAKE
BAKE THE PIES UNTIL GOLDEN BROWN, ABOUT 20-25 MINUTES.

06   07

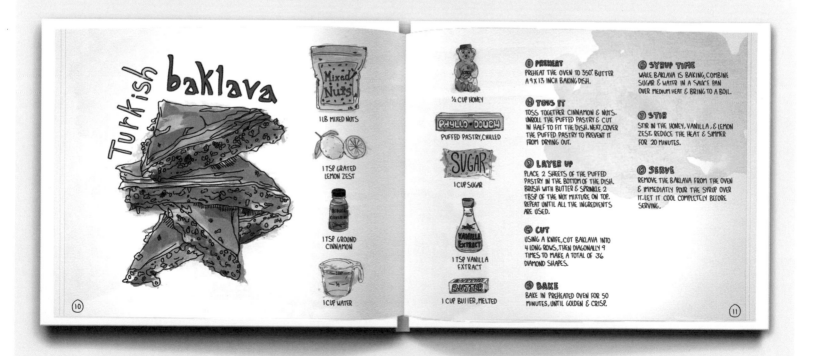

Turkish baklava

Ingredients:

- 1 LB MIXED NUTS
- 1 TSP GRATED LEMON ZEST
- 1 TSP GROUND CINNAMON
- 1 CUP WATER
- ½ CUP HONEY
- PHYLLO DOUGH / PUFFED PASTRY, CHILLED
- 1 CUP SUGAR
- 1 TSP VANILLA EXTRACT
- 1 CUP BUTTER, MELTED

① PREHEAT
PREHEAT THE OVEN TO 350°. BUTTER A 9 X 13 INCH BAKING DISH.

② TOSS IT
TOSS TOGETHER CINNAMON & NUTS. UNROLL THE PUFFED PASTRY & CUT IN HALF TO FIT THE DISH. NEXT, COVER THE PUFFED PASTRY TO PREVENT IT FROM DRYING OUT.

③ LAYER UP
PLACE 2 SHEETS OF THE PUFFED PASTRY IN THE BOTTOM OF THE DISH. BRUSH WITH BUTTER & SPRINKLE 2 TBSP OF THE NUT MIXTURE ON TOP. REPEAT UNTIL ALL THE INGREDIENTS ARE USED.

④ CUT
USING A KNIFE, CUT BAKLAVA INTO 4 LONG ROWS, THEN DIAGONALLY 9 TIMES TO MAKE A TOTAL OF 36 DIAMOND SHAPES.

⑤ BAKE
BAKE IN PREHEATED OVEN FOR 50 MINUTES, UNTIL GOLDEN & CRISP.

⑥ SYRUP TIME
WHILE BAKLAVA IS BAKING, COMBINE SUGAR & WATER IN A SAUCE PAN OVER MEDIUM HEAT & BRING TO A BOIL.

⑦ STIR
STIR IN THE HONEY, VANILLA, & LEMON ZEST. REDUCE THE HEAT & SIMMER FOR 20 MINUTES.

⑧ SERVE
REMOVE THE BAKLAVA FROM THE OVEN & IMMEDIATELY POUR THE SYRUP OVER IT. LET IT COOL COMPLETELY BEFORE SERVING.

10   11

¾ CUP & 2 TBSP
MATZO MEAL

3 TBSP
VEGETABLE OIL

1 5-LB CHICKEN, CUT IN PIECES

PEPPER

3 PARSNIPS
PEELED & SLICED

3 EGGS

1½ TSP SALT

10 CUPS
CHICKEN STOCK

CELERY
STALK

FRESH DILL

3 CARROTS, SLICED

Matzo Ball Soup

① WHISK IT
IN A MEDIUM BOWL, WHISK THE EGGS, CHICKEN STOCK, ½ CUP WATER, & SALT TOGETHER. NEXT, ADD THE MATZO MEAL, WHISK UNTIL COMBINED. COVER & COOL THE BATTER UNTIL FIRM.

② BOIL
LINE A BAKING PAN WITH PARCHMENT. BRING THE CHICKEN & THE STOCK TO A BOIL. REDUCE HEAT TO SIMMER.

③ FORM BALLS
FORM 2 HEAPING TABLESPOONS OF BATTER INTO A 1½-INCH BALL & PLACE THE BALL ON THE PAN & REPEAT STEPS.

④ ADD VEGGIES
NEXT, SLIDE THE MATZO BALLS INTO THE STOCK & COVER FOR 10 MINUTES. ADD CARROTS & PARSNIPS & CONTINUE COOKING FOR 25 MINUTES.

⑤ SERVE
TO SERVE, FILL THE BOWLS EVENLY WITH SOUP & VEGETABLES. PLACE 2 MATZO BALLS IN EACH BOWL & GARNISH WITH FRESH DILL.

12

13

1 CUP SOUR CREAM

14 OZ CAN WHOLE PEELED TOMATOES

6 GARLIC CLOVES, FINELY CHOPPED

CHOPPED CILANTRO

SALT

2 LB GROUND BEEF

1 SMALL ONION, CHOPPED

2 TBSP OLIVE OIL DIVIDED

12 OZ BOTTLE OF CHILI SAUCE

1 TBSP GARLIC POWDER

3 TBSP CHILE POWDER

¼ CUP WORCESTERSHIRE SAUCE

1 TBSP ONION POWDER

1 TBSP BROWN SUGAR

1 TBSP GROUND CUMIN

SHREDDED CHEDDAR CHEESE

CHUNKY SALSA

12 TACO SHELLS

2 AVOCADOS

LETTUCE

MEXICAN TACOS

❶ COOK THE MEAT
HEAT 1 TABLESPOON OF THE OIL IN A SKILLET OVER MEDIUM HEAT. COOK THE BEEF UNTIL COOKED THROUGH. ABOUT 5 MINUTES.

❷ TRANSFER
REMOVE FROM HEAT TO A LARGE BOWL.

❸ VEGGIE TIME
HEAT THE REMAINING 1 TABLESPOON IN THE SKILLET & ADD ONIONS & GARLIC. STIR UNTIL THEY BEGIN TO TURN BROWN.

❹ PREHEAT
PREHEAT OVEN TO 400° & ADD THE TOMATOES TO THE SKILLET FOR 10 MINUTES OR UNTIL IT THICKENS.

❺ MIX
THEN ADD IN THE BEEF, CHILI & WORCESTERSHIRE SAUCES, CHILE, GARLIC, & ONION POWDERS, SUGAR, & CUMIN.

❻ BAKE
COOK & STIR FOR ABOUT 10-12 MINUTES UNTIL WELL MIXED. NEXT SPREAD THE MIXTURE EVENLY IN 13X9X2" BAKING DISH, BAKE UNTIL A CRUST FORMS, FOR 30-90 MINUTES.

❼ SERVE
SERVE FILLING IN SHELLS & ENJOY WITH TOPPINGS & CHIPS.

16

17

Udon
うどん

1 PREP BROTH
IN A MEDIUM SAUCEPAN, ADD 3 CUPS OF WATER & A DASHI PACKET. BRING TO A BOIL & DISCARD THE PACKET.

2 ADD SEASONINGS
WHILE THE BROTH IS AT A SIMMER, ADD THE SOY SAUCE, SUGAR, & SALT.

3 STIR
STIR IN THE NOODLES FOR 6 MINUTES.

4 SERVE
SERVE IN A BOWL WITH GREEN ONION, THINLY SLICED NARUTOMAKI, INARIAGE (CUT IN HALF), & BLANCHED SPINACH. ADDITIONAL TOPPINGS MAYBE ADDED.

14

2 TBSP SOY SAUCE

BLANCHED SPINACH, CHOPPED

2 TSP SUGAR

1" GREEN ONION, FINELY SLICED

4 CUPS DASHI

2 PACKAGES OF UDON

3 CUPS WATER

1 NARUTOMAKI (FISH CAKE) THINLY SLICED

inariage (FRIED TOFU)
2 INARIAGE

½ TSP SALT

15

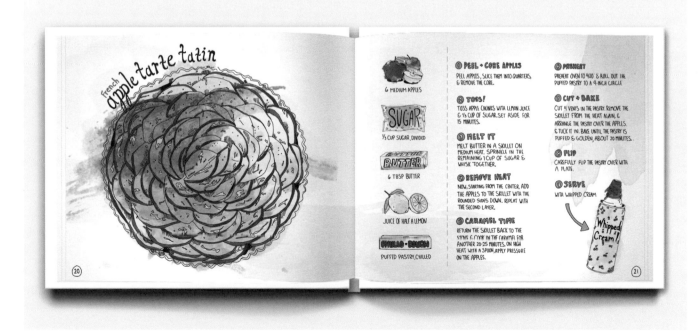

French apple tarte tatin

6 MEDIUM APPLES

SUGAR
⅓ CUP SUGAR, DIVIDED

BUTTER
6 TBSP BUTTER

JUICE OF HALF A LEMON

PUFFED PASTRY, CHILLED

1 PEEL + CORE APPLES
PEEL APPLES, SLICE THEM INTO QUARTERS, & REMOVE THE CORE.

2 TOSS!
TOSS APPLE CHUNKS WITH LEMON JUICE & ⅓ CUP OF SUGAR. SET ASIDE FOR 15 MINUTES.

3 MELT IT
MELT BUTTER IN A SKILLET ON MEDIUM HEAT. SPRINKLE IN THE REMAINING 1 CUP OF SUGAR & WHISK TOGETHER.

4 REMOVE HEAT
NOW, STARTING FROM THE CENTER, ADD THE APPLES TO THE SKILLET WITH THE ROUNDED SIDES DOWN. REPEAT WITH THE SECOND LAYER.

5 CARAMEL TIME
RETURN THE SKILLET BACK TO THE STOVE & COOK IN THE CARAMEL FOR ANOTHER 20-25 MINUTES. ON HIGH HEAT WITH A SPOON, APPLY PRESSURE ON THE APPLES.

6 PREHEAT
PREHEAT OVEN TO 400° & ROLL OUT THE PUFFED PASTRY TO A 9-INCH CIRCLE

7 CUT + BAKE
CUT 4 VENTS IN THE PASTRY. REMOVE THE SKILLET FROM THE HEAT AGAIN, & ARRANGE THE PASTRY OVER THE APPLES, & TUCK IT IN. BAKE UNTIL THE PASTRY IS PUFFED & GOLDEN, ABOUT 20 MINUTES.

8 FLIP
CAREFULLY FLIP THE PASTRY OVER WITH A PLATE.

9 SERVE
WITH WHIPPED CREAM

Whipped Cream

20

21

Cookbook
for Children

- **Designers**
  Alona Baranova, Olga Drach

- **Material**
  Photo Paper

- **Size**
  232mm x 238mm

- **Completion**
  2015

- **Photo Credit**
  Drach Evgeniya

This book was created in response to recommendations by pediatricians for healthy baby food and the need to diversify children's diets. It contains simple dishes that will appeal to babies and toddlers and to the parents who cook their food. It focuses on meals that are not easily bought in supermarkets or elsewhere.

Production of the book took place in several stages. Once the final list of recipes to be included was approved, photography of the dishes took place. Images are divided into two parts—the finished dish and what happens to the dish after mixing it in a blender. The designer collaborated with an artist, who made suggestions to improve the layout, and also came up with pictorial ideas including a big-eyed vegetable, funny fish and a cabbage in a panic!

Chinatown Kitchen

- **Collaborators**
  Lizzie Mabbott (Author),
  Yasia Williams-Leedham
  (Designer),
  Abigail Read (Illustrator)

- **Size**
  189mm x 246mm

- **Completion**
  2015

- **Photo Credit**
  David Munns

- **Publisher**
  Mitchell Beazley

Southeast Asian food is more popular than ever before, but some people may be put off cooking it because they're not familiar with the ingredients. *Chinatown Kitchen*'s author Lizzie Mabbott addresses this challenge by identifying key ingredients in Southeast Asian cooking and explaining the differences between the 77 types of noodles and how to cook them.

Designer Yasia Williams-Leedham wanted to create a scrapbook feel for this book. She seamlessly combined illustration with photography, and fully integrated the typography into the design spread by spread. She often used the photography to inform the illustration, extending parts of the photographs into illustrations on opposite pages, or drawing on top of the images.

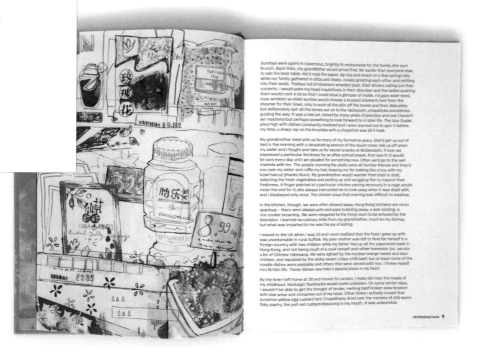

MAKES 10-15 ROLLS

1 Combine the noodles, lettuce, carrot and coriander in a bowl and mix together well.

Mix the sauce ingredients together in a suitable bowl until well combined.

Prepare a bowl of hand-hot water. Lay out a clean, dry tea towel in front of you.

few seconds – it should start softening up. Remove from the water and lay out flat on the tea towel.

nearer the bottom closest to you. Top with a tablespoon of crab or pork etc (if using).

Fold the bottom flap over the filling, tucking it under the filling a little.

Then fold the 2 sides in thirds.

prawn halves horizontally in a row on the empty wrapper above the filling.

Place seam side down, under a damp tea towel, while you prepare the rest.

Fold the whole thing over again. The wrapper should be tacky enough to stick to itself.

Place a couple of chives so that they sit in line horizontally with the pouch of filling but so that they will poke out of the side.

VIETNAMESE SUMMER ROLLS

Rice paper is the Vietnamese version of a spring roll wrapper. Sold dried in rounds, rice paper is brittle and fragile when dry, yet supple and elastic once softened in water. Summer rolls use the rice paper in its softened state, while spring rolls go a step further with a little deep-frying action.

20g (¾oz) bundle of dried rice vermicelli noodles, soaked in just-boiled water for 8 minutes and then drained, rinsed and cut into 7.5cm (3in) lengths

1 small head of Little Gem lettuce, shredded

1 carrot, peeled and julienned

100g (3½oz) picked white crab meat or leftover cooked shredded pork, chicken or duck (optional)

small handful of fresh coriander, finely chopped

10–15 summer roll wrappers (skins)

10 large cooked peeled prawns, sliced in half lengthways

a few sprigs of mint, leaves picked

bundle of chives

For the dipping sauce:

2 tbsp hoi sin sauce

1 tbsp Homemade Sriracha (see page 109, or use shop-bought) or chilli oil

1 tsp smooth peanut butter

1 tbsp rice vinegar

½ tbsp water

Serve the rolls with the dipping sauce, or alternatively with Nuoc Cham (see page 34).

FLAT EGG NOODLES

...in bundles, these are great tossed with a dressing, salad or stir-fried. Cook in simmering water for minutes until the bundle has relaxed, then drain well with a little cooking oil to prevent them from sticking.

HONG KONG NOODLES
(WONTON NOODLES OR LO MEIN)

...in the chiller cabinet, these are often tossed with... 'lo mein' ('lo' means 'mix it up' and mein means 'noodle', so... to this method of preparation specifically) or used in... soups. Refresh in boiling water for 1 minute to remove... of the flour on the surface of the noodles, drain and... with cold water, then plunge back into boiling water... to warm them before dressing. You can also buy these... convenience, and the top-quality versions contain... (prawn) roe – you will see tiny dots of it in each noodle. Cook the noodles by simmering in boiling water for minutes, then drain but keep the water the noodles were in for dipping the noodles into or sipping on the side. The water is flavoured with the shrimp roe.

SHANGHAI NOODLES
UDON

...noodles, usually found in the fridge section, are... eaten, which are Japanese wheat noodles. They are... more square and sometimes round and thicker than... noodles. Hence people often saying they resemble worms. They are satisfying udon are the frozen or vacuum-cooked... but they are also sold dry. Heat through with boiling... until the udon cake has loosened, then drain and dress... noodle soups or stir-fry. Whereas udon are eaten both... warm and cold with a dipping sauce, Shanghai noodles... stir-fried and served hot.

(9 & 10) GLASS NOODLES
(BEAN THREAD OR CELLOPHANE) &
MUNG BEAN SHEET NOODLES

There are two main types of these noodles, made either with mung bean starch (9) or sweet potato starch (10). Both are used in braised dishes, salads, spring rolls and soups, though the sweet potato variety, used more commonly in Korean cooking, is thicker and has a chewier texture. Smooth, slippery and jelly-like, glass noodles are so-named for their see-through quality. Mung bean sheets are noodles made from the same starch but in varying widths, and can sometimes come in sheets for you to break off as you see fit. Soak in hot water for 10–30 minutes, depending on width, before using.

(11) SOBA (BUCKWHEAT) NOODLES

Soba noodles are always thin, and the Japanese eat them hot, cold, in soup or with a dipping sauce. In Korea, they are almost always eaten cold in the summertime. Cook as per the packet instructions, then rinse and refresh in iced water.

E-FU (YI MEIN)

These egg noodles are round and sold deep-fried into flat discs about the size of your palm. They have a spongy texture when cooked, and are often eaten at birthdays for longevity, since the noodles themselves are always long strands, symbolizing long life. These are most commonly eaten in restaurants, with luxury ingredients such as lobster and crab.

RAMEN

Chinese in origin, ramen noodles are now often synonymous with the Japanese noodle soup dish. They are wheat noodles made with alkaline water to give them elasticity and come in thick or thin, wavy or straight varieties, depending on the type of ramen broth they're destined for. Instant noodles, since they mostly come in soup, are often called instant ramen.

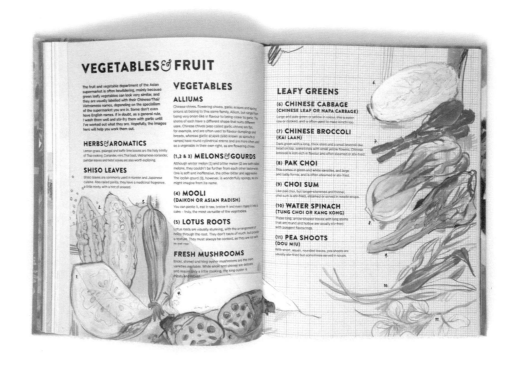

VEGETABLES & FRUIT

The fruit and vegetable department of the Asian supermarket is often bewildering, mainly because green leafy vegetables can look very similar, and they are usually labelled with their Chinese/Thai/Vietnamese names, depending on the specialism of the supermarket you are in. Some don't even have English names. If in doubt, as a general rule, I wash them and stir-fry them with garlic until I've worked out what they are. Hopefully, the images here will help you work them out.

HERBS & AROMATICS

Lemon grass, galangal and kaffir lime leaves are the holy trinity of Thai making. Coriander, mint, Thai basil, Vietnamese coriander, pandan leaves and betel leaves are also worth exploring.

SHISO LEAVES

Shiso leaves are commonly used in Korean and Japanese cuisine. Also called perilla, they have a medicinal fragrance, a little minty, with a hint of aniseed.

VEGETABLES

ALLIUMS

Chinese chives, flowering chives, garlic scapes and spring onions all belong to this same family. Allium, but range from being very onion-like in flavour to being closer to garlic. The stems of each have a different shape that suits different uses. Chinese chives (also called garlic chives) are flat, for example, and are often used to flavour dumplings and breads, whereas garlic scapes (also known as sprouts or ramps) have round cylindrical stems and are more often used as a vegetable in their own right, as are flowering chives

(1, 2 & 3) MELONS & GOURDS

Although winter melon (1) and bitter melon (2) are both called melons, they couldn't be further from each other tastewise. One is soft and inoffensive, the other bitter and aggressive. The loofah gourd (3), however, is wonderfully spongy, as you might imagine from its name.

(4) MOOLI
(DAIKON OR ASIAN RADISH)

You can pickle it, eat it raw, braise it and even make it into a cake – truly, the most versatile of the vegetables.

(5) LOTUS ROOTS

Lotus roots are visually stunning, with the arrangement of holes through the root. They don't taste of much, but provide a texture. They must always be cooked, as they are not safe to eat raw.

FRESH MUSHROOMS

Enoki, shimeji and king oyster mushrooms are the main varieties available. White enoki and shimeji are delicate and resemble a little cooking, the king oyster is meaty and robust.

LEAFY GREENS

(6) CHINESE CABBAGE
(CHINESE LEAF OR NAPA CABBAGE)

Large and pale green or yellow in colour, this is eaten raw or cooked, and is often used to make kimchi too.

(7) CHINESE BROCCOLI
(KAI LAAN)

Dark green with a long, thick stem and a small broccoli-like head on top, sometimes with small yellow flowers, Chinese broccoli is iron-rich in flavour and often steamed or stir-fried.

(8) PAK CHOI

This comes in green and white varieties, and large and baby forms, and is often steamed or stir-fried.

(9) CHOI SUM

Like pak choi, but longer-stemmed and thinner, choi sum is stir-fried, steamed or served in noodle soups.

(10) WATER SPINACH
(TUNG CHOI OR KANG KONG)

These long, arrow-shaped leaves with long stems that are round and hollow are usually stir-fried with pungent flavourings.

(11) PEA SHOOTS
(DOU MIU)

With short, square, rounded leaves, pea shoots are usually stir-fried but sometimes served in soups.

(12) MUSTARD GREENS
(GAI CHOY)

These are what you would find pickled (see page 162). They have a bit of a spicy bite to them. You can pickle them yourself, braise them or add them to soups.

(13) CHRYSANTHEMUM GREENS (TONG HO)

These flat, rounded leaves are slightly bitter and medicinal in flavour, and are often used in hot pots and soups.

(14) RED / GREEN AMARANTH

The red amaranth leaves are easily distinguishable since they have a red tinge on the underside of the leaf. Sturdy and iron-rich, the green version is often used in soups, though the red is reserved for stir-frying, as the colour inside them releases a vibrant pink juice.

(15) MIZUNA

Used mostly in Japanese cooking, mizuna leaves are delicate and long, and spiked at the edges. They taste a bit like rocket.

HOW I LIKE TO EAT LEAFY GREENS

In Soup (noodle soup, broths, stews): Chinese cabbage, pea shoots, chrysanthemum greens, pak choi, choi sum, mustard greens, green amaranth, mizuna

Stir-fried with ginger: Chinese broccoli (boil in water with 1 tsp sugar for 2 minutes, then stir-fry)

Stir-fried with garlic: Pea shoots, pak choi, Chinese cabbage, red / green amaranth

Stir-fried with garlic & fermented bean curd: Water spinach, Chinese broccoli (boil in water with 1 tsp sugar for 2 minutes, then stir-fry)

Steamed & drizzled with oyster sauce: Pak choi, choi sum, Chinese broccoli

Raw: Chinese cabbage, mizuna

FRUIT

(16) MANGOSTEEN

Often called the 'queen of fruits', mangosteens are little purple spheres and are one of my favourite fruits. Squeeze the rind until the fruit splits, then pull apart to reveal the soft white flesh inside. The larger globes may have a seed in them which you can spit out. Soft, creamy and fragrant, these don't come cheap when imported, but are incredibly delicious.

(17) RAMBUTAN

These are distinctive from their red, hairy outer shells. Crack the skin open and pop the fruit in your mouth, but there is a seed in the centre you will need to spit out.

(18) LONGANS

Called 'dragon's eye' in Cantonese, these are similar in size to lychees, but are beige and smooth-skinned. Pop the skin open with your teeth after washing them, then peel the skin away to reveal the flesh.

(19) LYCHEES

Pink-skinned and a little knobbly, lychees need to be peeled before eating and stoned. Purée the fruit and reduce to a syrup to flavour drinks, or ice the lychee flesh and eat with ice cream.

(20) ASIAN PEARS

These are yellow and round, the skin is thin and the flesh has an almost icy texture to it. Not a great deal of flavour other than sweetness, but one of my trusted hangover alleviators.

(21) DRAGONFRUIT

It's a dramatic-looking fruit, with pink skin and black-seeded, snow-white flesh. The skin should not be eaten. To prepare, slice the fruit in half and scoop the white flesh out with a large spoon.

(22) PAPAYA

Long and oval-shaped, ripe papayas are orange-fleshed. They're my least favourite fruit; they're a bit too reminiscent of rotting fruit. I can just about bear them with a squeeze of lime. To make classic Thai salads, go for unripe and green fruits.

(23) MANGO

Mangoes are now so easily available you can buy them in most general supermarkets. Alphonso mangos, available for a short season, are some of the best: honey-like in flavour and creamy. Many Indian and Caribbean grocers sell mango purée in tins.

(24) DURIAN

Often called the 'king of fruits', durian is infamous for its god-awful smell. Banned in many hotels and public transport in Asia, durian is pretty good once you get past the odour. The fruit itself is encased in a hard, spiked shell; once you get it open, bright yellow lobes of creamy flesh can be eaten, made into ice cream, cakes and candies. You can often find the lobes frozen or in the fridge section of the supermarket.

Garlic scapes (also called sprouts or ramps) are the sturdiest of the allium family that you can find in Chinatown. The stems are round and thick, smelling pungently of garlic that mellows out in cooking, and can take a fair bit of heat. If you can't find them, use spring onions or Chinese chives instead (see page 82), and reduce the cooking time.

SERVES 2 AS A SIDE DISH

GARLIC SCAPES STIR-FRIED
with PRAWNS & EGG

Mix the soy sauce with the cornflour in a bowl, stir in the prawns and leave to marinate while you prepare the rest of the dish.

Beat the eggs in another bowl with the black pepper, white pepper, salt and rice wine. Cut the garlic scapes into 4cm (1½in) lengths.

Heat a wok on a medium heat and swirl 1 tablespoon of the cooking oil around it. When it is shimmering, add the garlic scapes and stir-fry for a good 5 minutes so that they take on some colour and soften. Turn the heat up to max and add the prawns, stir-frying them with the scapes for 30 seconds so that they turn a little pink. Push to one side and add the remaining tablespoon of cooking oil.

Pour in the eggs and leave for 10 seconds to set, then scramble into the prawns and scapes with a spatula. Take off the heat so that the eggs remain soft and creamy, then serve with some rice or noodles.

1 tsp light soy sauce
1 tsp cornflour
200g (7oz) uncooked peeled king prawns
4 free-range eggs
pinch of ground black pepper
pinch of ground white pepper
pinch of salt
1 tbsp Shaoxing rice wine
4 stalks of garlic scapes
2 tbsp cooking oil
splash of sesame oil

▶▶ OTHER IDEAS

Stir-fry the garlic scapes with thinly sliced marinated meat, tofu (bean curd) or mushrooms, make pastes with them or shred them raw and add to the dressing for the Smacked Cucumber Salad (see page 33)

There is just a hint of seasoning here, since the garlic scapes and the bacon are so aromatic on their own. The garlic scapes are like a grassy, sweeter garlic and are robust when raw; mellow when cooked. I especially enjoy the flavour of them when they are a little charred. Like a lot of dishes in Asian cuisines, just a little bit of meat is needed to impart flavour rather than to dominate. I often eat this with just a bowl of rice.

SERVES 4 AS A SIDE DISH

THAI-STYLE GARLIC SCAPES
STIR-FRIED with BACON

Wash your garlic scapes thoroughly, pat dry with kitchen paper and then chop into 5cm (2in) lengths. Slice the bacon rashers into slivers.

Heat the oil in a wok on a high heat until just below smoking. Add the bacon and stir-fry until some of the fat has rendered and the bacon is starting to crisp.

Turn the heat up to max and add the garlic scapes. Stir-fry briskly for 3 minutes, then add the fish sauce, sugar and white pepper. Stir-fry for another minute, then take off the heat and spoon out on to a plate.

400g (14oz) garlic scapes (sprouts) (see page 82)
6 rashers of smoked streaky bacon
1 tbsp cooking oil
1 tbsp fish sauce
1 tsp sugar
½ tsp ground white pepper

The joy of these buns is in their fried bottoms. Steamed buns can at times be a bit too pillowy and sweet; in frying these, they become crunchy with a fluffy top. In my eagerness to eat them, I invariably burn my mouth and dribble pork juices down my chin. At least it's never dull.

PORK PRESERVED VEGETABLE BUNS

MAKES **12**

For the dough:
200g (7oz) strong white flour, plus extra for dusting
100g (3½oz) plain flour
1 tsp fast-action dried yeast
2½ tbsp sugar
a small tsp salt
2 tbsp cooking oil
175ml (6fl oz) water

For the filling:
3 leaves of Chinese cabbage (Chinese leaf or Napa cabbage)
1 tbsp fine salt
50g (1¾oz) Tianjin preserved vegetable (see page 162)
2.5cm (1in) slice of fresh root ginger, peeled
1 spring onion
280g (10oz) fatty minced pork (fat is important here, as you want the insides to be juicy)
2 tsp light soy sauce
2 tsp sesame oil
1 tsp sugar
pinch of ground white pepper
1 tsp cornflour
1 tbsp cooking oil, plus a little extra for frying a sample of the filling to check the seasoning

For the dipping sauce:
1 tbsp Chinkiang black vinegar
½ tbsp water
pinch of sugar
1 tbsp chilli oil

Combine all the ingredients for the dough, except the water, in a mixing bowl, then add the water bit by bit until you get a soft dough, mixing thoroughly. Knead by hand on a lightly floured work surface, or using an electric mixer fitted with a dough hook, for 5 minutes until smooth. Put it back into the bowl, cover it with clingfilm and leave to rise in a warm place for an hour.

While the dough is rising, make up the filling. Slice the cabbage leaves in half lengthways and chop finely. Add to a colander and sprinkle with the fine salt. Leave over a bowl or the sink for 20 minutes for all the water to drain out.

Meanwhile, add the preserved vegetable to a large bowl of water to rinse some of the salt out. Leave this for 20 minutes too.

Chop the ginger and spring onion very finely and add to the pork with the soy sauce, sesame oil, sugar, pepper and cornflour. Mix with chopsticks in one direction until all is well amalgamated.

Rinse the cabbage and drain well, then add to the pork mixture. Rinse the preserved vegetable and chop roughly, then also add to the pork. Mix together well. Fry a teaspoonful of the mixture in a little cooking oil in a nonstick frying pan and taste to check the seasoning.

Tip the risen dough on to a floured work surface. Knead lightly a couple of times, then roll into a sausage shape and cut into 12 even pieces.

Press down on each piece of dough to form into a rough circle.

Roll the circle out to the size of your palm. It's preferable to have the middle a little thicker than the edges.

Add about a tablespoon of filling to each circle.

Then start gathering in the sides of the dough.

Twist until you have sealed the bun. Give the seal a pinch to ensure it's properly closed.

You should end up with a neatly sealed bun. Place the buns on a floured plate while you make the rest.

To cook, heat the oil in the nonstick frying pan and fry the buns flat side down. When the bottoms are browned, add a few splashes of water and put the lid on to steam them. Repeat a couple of times for about 8 minutes until cooked through. While the buns are steaming, mix the dipping sauce ingredients together in a serving bowl. Serve the buns hot with the dipping sauce.

...fresh water melon
...dried shrimps
...onion, diagonally sliced,
...d green parts separated
...eeled and chopped fresh root ginger
...ch of salt
...fl oz) water
...ground white pepper

...NTER MELON BRAISED ...DRIED SHRIMPS

SERVES **4**

...er melon, used most often in soups, tastes of ...ttle, so one might ask why we don't just feed it ...pigs? Because it has a wonderful texture that ...t and non-fibrous, and it has a way of soaking ...the flavours around it.

...winter melon using a vegetable ...en cut into thick matchsticks.

...d dried shrimps and then soak ...of hot water for 2 minutes. ...leave to one side.

...ok up on a high heat and add ...ing oil, swirling it to coat the ...d the whites of the spring onion ...inger and stir-fry over the high ...about 20 seconds until fragrant. ...soaked shrimps and winter ...ticks and stir-fry for 2 minutes.

...salt, water and white pepper ...ry until the water has ...ed. Turn off the heat and taste ...the seasoning, then serve in ...uls garnished with the sliced ...ion greens.

VEGETABLES *and* FRUIT 97

HOW TO PREPARE PINEAPPLE *the* ASIAN WAY

The pineapple is an interesting fruit; it is one of the rare ones that works in both sweet and savoury dishes. There's an enzyme in pineapple that tenderises meat, which is why it sometimes tickles your tongue when you bite into it; it is, effectively, biting you back. If you've ever been to Thailand or the Philippines or indeed Mexico, you might, as I was, be blown away by the skill and dexterity with which the street vendors strip a pineapple of its skin and eyes to create chunks of sweet, juicy fruit ready to eat without having to spit anything out or have any of it stuck in your teeth. A few sharp hacks of a large knife (or a machete, but let's stick to a knife) is all it takes.

In choosing your pineapple, give it a good sniff at the base of the fruit. People may look at you askance, but a ripe pineapple will smell so. Also, give the green leaves nearest the centre of the fruit a little tug; a ripe fruit will release them easily.

Twist the pineapple crown and store (too) from the top of the green leaves, slice the skin off close to the flesh to reveal the 'eyes' all the way out.

Holding the pineapple with your left hand, you will see that the eyes sit in a diagonal row. Make an incision with your knife at a 45-degree angle from above the first eye, slice the skin off on either side so that the eyes come away cleanly. Repeat down the pineapple to the first row, then turn the pineapple round and repeat. As the eyes have been cut out, example, to the starting point will reset the end.

Cut the quarters in half, and then slice out the hard, woody centre. It's now ready to eat, or you can cut it into smaller bite-sized pieces.

Now take the top and bottom off. Rinse the pineapple, then cut it in half lengthways and then in half again.

118 VEGETABLES *and* FRUIT

MAKES ENOUGH FOR 1 CUT PINEAPPLE

This chilli, sugar and salt dip comes in a little bag with fruit purchased from street vendors in Thailand. It's fantastic with very sweet fruit, but also with acidic fruit like green apple, as the sugar balances it out a little. Green mango, pineapple, cantaloupe melon and watermelon work really well with this, and sometimes I crush in a few mint leaves for a little variation.

CHILLI SUGAR SALT DIP

1 large red chilli
1 tbsp fine salt
2 tbsp caster sugar

Slice the chilli in half lengthways and scoop the seeds out with a teaspoon. Slice thinly into half rings and place in a mortar. Add the salt and sugar and pound lightly with a pestle, tainting the sugar and salt mixture pink.

VEGETABLES *and* FRUIT 119

Fashion & Food

- **Design Agency**
  Julia Janus

- **Designers**
  Paulius Budrikis,
  Benjaminas Alimas

- **Printing Technology**
  Hot Stamping and Foiling

- **Size**
  250mm x 320mm

- **Completion**
  2015

- **Photo Credit**
  Rokas Baltakys

- **Publisher**
  Julia Janus

Fashion & Food is an interdisciplinary collaboration that connects the New Northern or Baltic gastronomy with fashion through visual dialogues. Three innovative restaurants and their chefs are involved with the book: Uoksas restaurant (Kàunas, Lithuania; chef Artūras Naidenko); Tres Pavars (Riga, Latvia; chefs Martins Sirmaisir and Eriks Dreibants); and Biblioteka No 1 (Riga; chef Maris Jansons).

The book explores the relationship between fashion (as a sociocultural phenomenon) and gastronomical identity in Baltic countries. Publisher Julia Janus uses the latest technology to explore these themes. Chefs involved in the project had the challenging task of providing recipes that matched the intensive magnetism of the clothing photographed for the book. Their dishes also had to be cooked with seasonal products from the Baltic region.

This book is slowly becoming a chronicle of fashion and food among modern northern European cultures.

CEPTAS
CIPE
ЦЕПТ

**...DYTAS ŠOKOLADINIS
...MAS (PRANC. *GANACHE*)
...BUROKINIU „STIKLU" ir
...FILIZUOTOMIS VYŠNIOMIS**

...orcijos

**FROZEN BLACK CHOCOLATE
GANACHE with BEETROOT
GLASS and LYOPHILIZED
CHERRIES**

6 servings

**МОРОЖЕНЫЙ ГАНАШ из
ЧЕРНОГО ШОКОЛАДА,
СВЕКОЛЬНОЕ СТЕКЛО,
ЛИОФИЛИЗИРОВАННАЯ
ВИШНЯ**

6 порций

18   24   Spring / Summer 2015   25

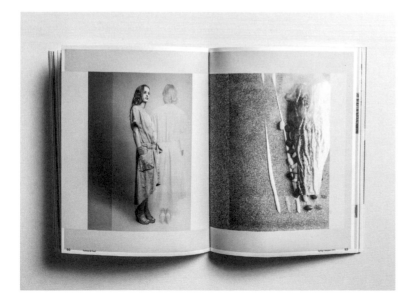

Culinary Design—Hand-Craft Edition

- **Designer**
  Julie Flogeac

- **Material**
  5mm Fibreboard, 135gsm Ink Jet Matt Coated Paper

- **Size**
  200mm x 400mm

- **Photo Credit**
  Julie Flogeac

This book was produced to present the work of culinary designer Stéphane Bureaux and to impart knowledge around his craft. Paper is manipulated in the book to reflect how Bureaux uses and crafts his food. His culinary artworks are presented on a white background, while vegetables are shot on a black background to contrast the book's different types of content and to create an immersive space.

The whole book, including the binding, is entirely handmade. It opens in two parts, like an accordion: Bureaux's food creations occupy the left-hand side of the book, while the black-background photos are printed on the right-hand side. Photos are partly hidden by a dramatic black perforated pattern. When the book is fully opened up, a fun pop-up creation emerges that readers can interact with.

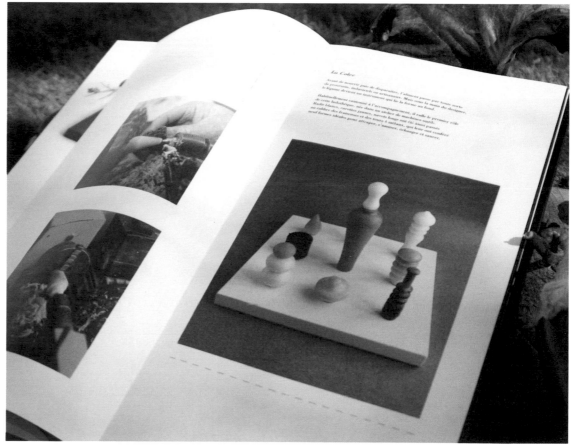

Malevich at My Table

- **Designer**
  Anna Hargitay

- **Material**
  140gsm Offset Paper,
  200gsm Matt Coated Paper

- **Size**
  200mm x 200mm

- **Completion**
  2015

- **Photo Credit**
  Dorottya Vékony

The primary purpose of this work was not to explore cooking per se, but to present a visual play on food. Seven days, seven menus is the theme and each day consists of a three-course lunch. Food servings, which were inspired by Polish–Russian artist Kazimir Malevich's works, were styled in a geometric form and each meal was photographed to stand on its own.

Designer Anna Hargitay stripped the meals of their original shape, so that individual components could not be identified. If someone was to eat these meals, they could only rely on their taste, as there would be no other way of recognizing what each dish was. In addition to the geometric shapes used when styling the dishes, color plays an important role in the design; the variation of these two elements (shape and color) contributes to a dynamic outcome.

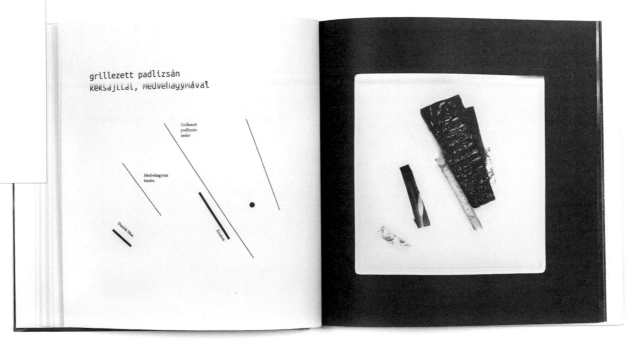

málna tetős citromos sajttorta
csokoládé öntettel

Zabkeksz összetörve vajjal elkeverve
████████████████████████
████████████████████████
vanília, citromlé, citromhéj). A krémet
a félig kész keksz lapra helyezve
készre sütni.
Málna szók cukorral és citrommal
kását felfőzve, majd zselatinnal
dermeszve.

Tejszínt felforralni abba keserű csokoládét darabolni. 2:1
arányban. Selymes fényűre
keverni.

Kezeletlen citrom héját
vízbe áztatva egy napig. A
vizet többször cserélni kell.
Cukorszirupban főzni, amíg
megváltozik az állaga és üve-
ges lesz, de nem kemény.

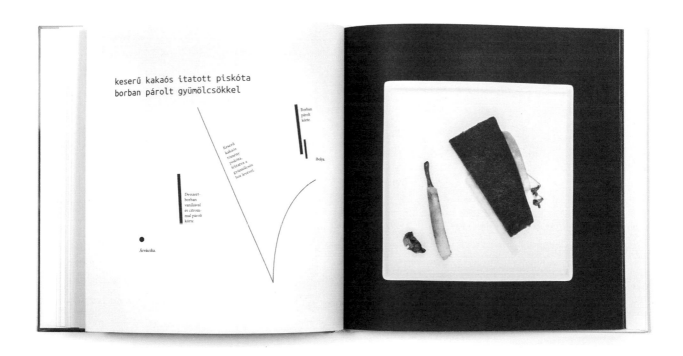

keserű kakaós itatott piskóta
borban párolt gyümölcsökkel

Borban
párolt
körte.

Keserű
kakaós
tömény
puncsot,
felitatva a
gyümölcsös
bor levével.

ibolya.

Desszert-
borban
vaníliával
és citrom-
mal párolt
körte

Árvácska.

6.NAP

A ZÖLD TRAPÉZ NAPJA

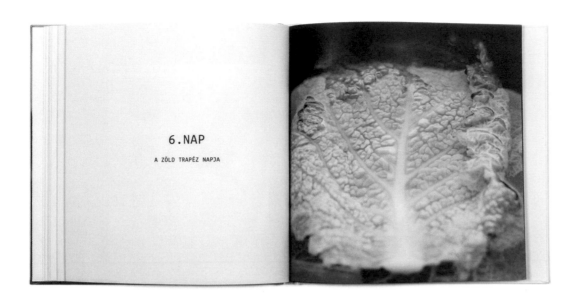

kivis túrótorta
szeder öntettel
grillázzsal

Szederlekvár citromlével ditszerve.

Grilláz tört törökmogyoróval

Vizes piskóta tésztán, citromos, citromhéjas, kevés mascarpone krémmel puhított, túrókrém, zsí trójssárgával cukorral és zselatinnal lett dermesztve. Vékonyra vágott kivivel díszítve a tetején.

sült oldalas
blansírozott káposztával
paprikás tejföllel

Pácolt csípős lével

Sörét tejjuszzsóban pácolt, rozsoml sült oldalas.

Paprikás tejföl egy csepp natúr tejföllel a közepen.

Savanyú lében blansírozott káposzta.

7.NAP

A PIROS AMORF NAPJA

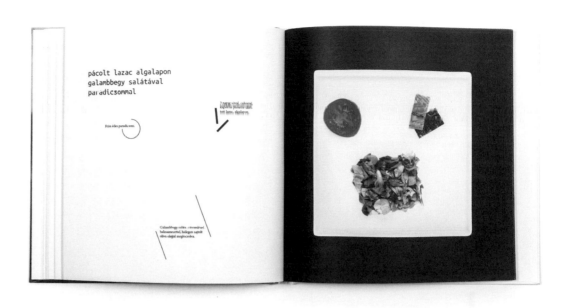

pácolt lazac algalapon
galambbegy salátával
paradicsommal

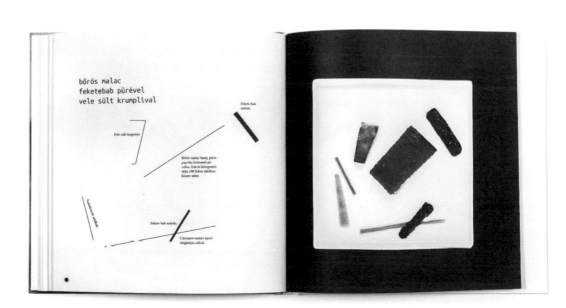

bőrös malac
feketebab pürével
vele sült krumplival

Endless Book

- **Designer**
  Dina Belenko

- **Material**
  Gloss Paper, Cardboard

- **Size**
  100mm x 300mm

- **Completion**
  2014

- **Photo Credit**
  Dina Belenko

Endless Book is the outcome of a year-long project for Dina Belenko. Every week for a year she took one photograph, bearing in mind one condition: the photo on the book's previous page should flow smoothly into the next one without visible seams or rough blends. At the end of the year she'd produced this large, panoramic book consisting of 52 images, which could be continued into the next year if she so desired.

The theme of the book is outer space created by still-life photos made from various foodstuffs, in particular coffee and sweets (sweet-toothed Belenko's main inspirations). As a still-life photographer, Belenko always tries to find something interesting in everyday objects: for this project, she found that marbled cookie dough could look like a constellation, a doughnut, the center of a star system, milk poured into coffee, a new-born galaxy. She also shot crop circles made of coffee beans, star-shaped biscuits and a big bang from a flour explosion.

Vale's Cookbook

- **Design Agency**
  Ampla Comunicação

- **Designer**
  Livia Hermanny

- **Material**
  Polished Pinus Wood,
  210gsm Matt Coated Paper,
  Metal Ring Binder

- **Size**
  200mm x 300mm

- **Completion**
  2015

- **Photo Credit**
  Jorge Sagrilo

This book showcases a collection of 27 recipes compiled by the employees of global mining company Vale, headquartered in Brazil. Its purpose was to share the recipes made from healthy and fresh ingredients, along with nutrition tips, among the company's workers.

With the intention of creating an unusual cookbook, the designer, Livia Hermanny, used a wooden board, similar to chopping boards found in a kitchen, as the back cover, which gives a rustic and different look to an object that's usually just made of paper. Pages are attached to the board via a metal ring binder on the left-hand side of the book, which references the regular binding of a book.

The design concept was mainly based on creating different patterns and shapes formed by photos of colorful ingredients.

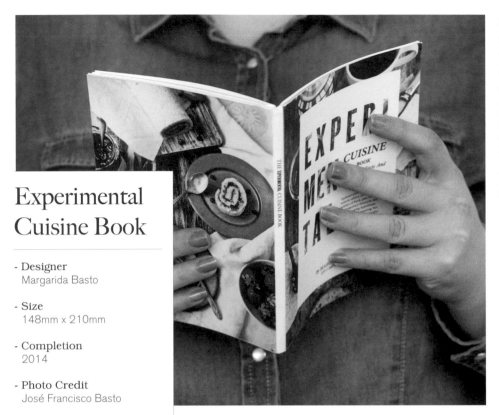

Experimental Cuisine Book

- **Designer**
  Margarida Basto

- **Size**
  148mm x 210mm

- **Completion**
  2014

- **Photo Credit**
  José Francisco Basto

Experimental Cuisine Book is an editorial artifact that explores and represents opposite but complementary food themes through the book material itself and contrasting graphic concepts. This briefing allowed the author/designer Margarida Basto to 'experiment' and play around with different visual concepts, materials and sizes in order to represent three topics covered in the book. She came up with a classical look for the 'The Science of Food' chapter, a contemporary design for 'Foods Today—The Foodpairing Hypothesis,' and an alternative and edgy design for the 'Antipairing' appendix.

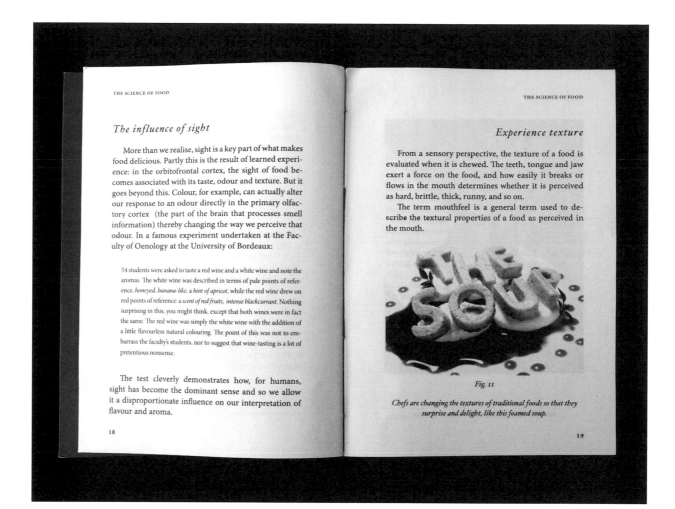

The influence of sight

More than we realise, sight is a key part of what makes food delicious. Partly this is the result of learned experience: in the orbitofrontal cortex, the sight of food becomes associated with its taste, odour and texture. But it goes beyond this. Colour, for example, can actually alter our response to an odour directly in the primary olfactory cortex (the part of the brain that processes smell information) thereby changing the way we perceive that odour. In a famous experiment undertaken at the Faculty of Oenology at the University of Bordeaux:

> 54 students were asked to taste a red wine and a white wine and note the aromas. The white wine was described in terms of pale points of reference, *honeyed, banana-like*, a *hint of apricot*, while the red wine drew on red points of reference: a *scent of red fruits, intense blackcurrant*. Nothing surprising in this, you might think, except that both wines were in fact the same. The red wine was simply the white wine with the addition of a little flavourless natural colouring. The point of this was not to embarrass the faculty's students, nor to suggest that wine-tasting is a lot of pretentious nonsense.

The test cleverly demonstrates how, for humans, sight has become the dominant sense and so we allow it a disproportionate influence on our interpretation of flavour and aroma.

18

Experience texture

From a sensory perspective, the texture of a food is evaluated when it is chewed. The teeth, tongue and jaw exert a force on the food, and how easily it breaks or flows in the mouth determines whether it is perceived as hard, brittle, thick, runny, and so on.

The term mouthfeel is a general term used to describe the textural properties of a food as perceived in the mouth.

Fig. 11

Chefs are changing the textures of traditional foods so that they surprise and delight, like this foamed soup.

19

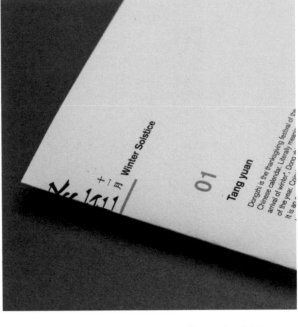

Seasons in Singapore

- **Designer**
  Jonathan Wee Chun Kiat

- **Material**
  Maple White RJ Paper

- **Size**
  220mm x 300mm

- **Completion**
  2014

People have long marked the change in seasons through observance and celebrations. Even in a tropical country like Singapore, where the seasons are less distinct, the Chinese still chart the seasons through the Chinese almanac and celebrate them by eating food that reflects changes within nature.

Seasons in Singapore is divided into five chapters that coincide with major Chinese festivals celebrated in Singapore. Each chapter has a different booklet that cascades down from one season to the next like a timeline. Twenty-four seasonal Chinese terms are incorporated into the design, along with a moon-phase icon that leads readers from the first month to the next. Colors of the seasons also act as a navigation tool through the different chapters of the book. There's a calendar attached to the book too, which allows readers to chart and follow the changes in food in line with nature.

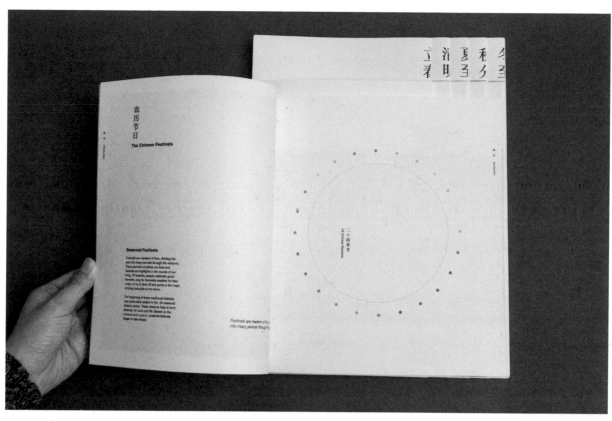

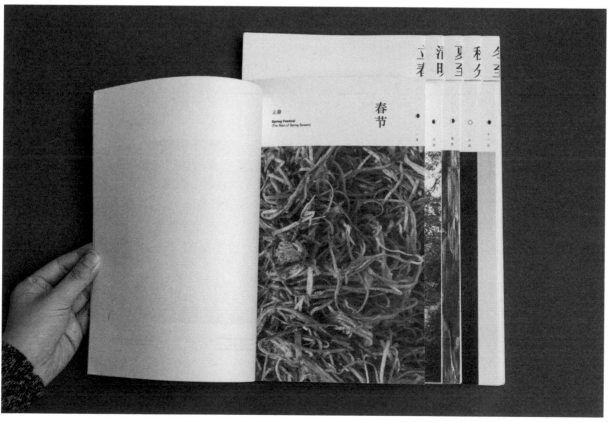

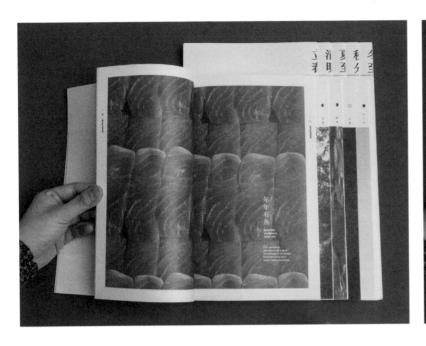

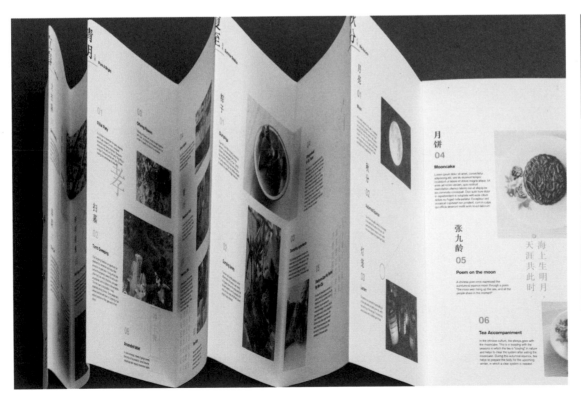

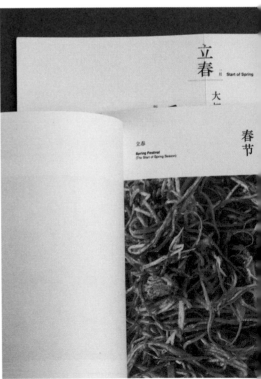

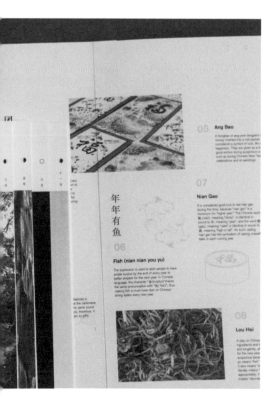

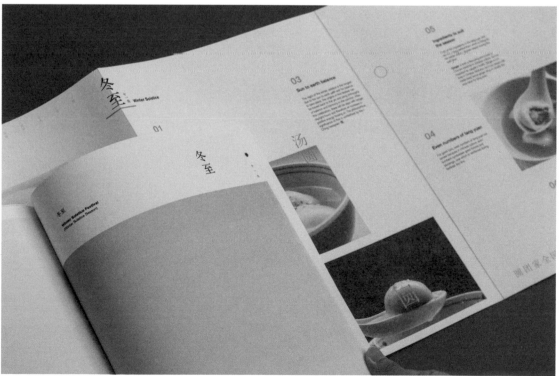

This recipe booklet is centered on designer Julia Chilcote's favorite thing to bake—cheesecake. Many cookbooks are very conventional in their design and layout, so Chilcote wanted to showcase cheesecake recipes in a different way. She did this by using fun, hand-drawn illustration for the ingredients and whimsical typesetting for the recipes. Enticing photography always makes recipes more appealing, and Chilcote baked and photographed every cheesecake in the book herself. She chose to include semicircular, die-cut pages for each recipe; when turned over, they reveal the recipe and an image of the cheesecake. The booklet has a simple saddle-stitched binding so that it can be inserted into a larger cookbook or magazine, or easily mailed.

Cheesecake Recipe Booklet

- **Designer**
  Julia Chilcote

- **Material**
  Semi-Gloss Text Paper

- **Size**
  152mm x 228mm

- **Completion**
  2015

- **Photo Credit**
  Julia Chilcote

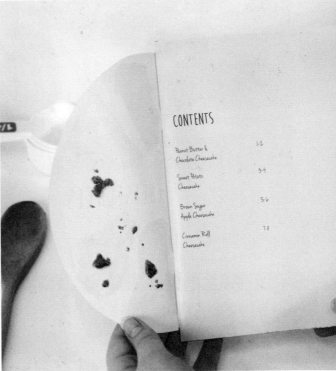

011

- **Designer**
  Renato Molnar

- **Material**
  Paper, Cardboard

- **Size**
  115mm x 160mm

- **Completion**
  2014

- **Photo Credit**
  Renato Molnar

The aim of this project was to collect different dishes that can be made with just a few ingredients/equipment, like what you might find in a bachelor pad or a dorm (the name *011* comes from the number of the room the meals were prepared in).

Divided into two parts by its content, one part describes the spices used during cooking, and the other contains 50 recipes and their photos (designer/photographer Renato Molnar is a firm believer in the power of an image to help someone decide what to cook). The spices are represented by vector-graphic illustrations; Molnar started out by sketching these on paper, but the final illustrations give the impression of a wood- or linocut.

Noticia Text is the font used for the body copy, and Molnar, who has a background in calligraphy, designed an additional font for the spice and recipe titles to add a personal touch to the book. Not surprisingly, his font has a calligraphic origin, so the first sketches were drawn with a flat-edged pen. Each letter has different versions, which helps to create more exciting visuals. Molnar used his knowledge of calligraphy to also create a variety of letter connections.

FŰSZEREK

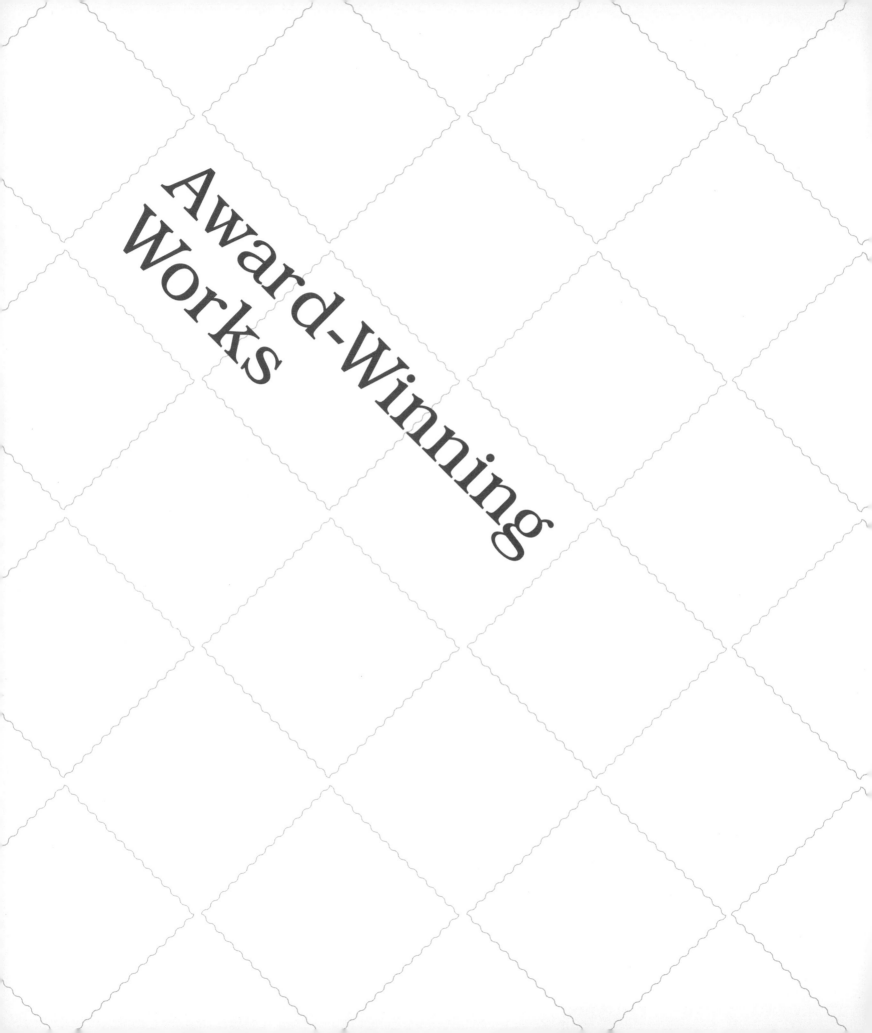

Award-Winning Works

Excellence in Cuisine Book Design

By Jens Mennicke

It is my pleasure to write the preface for this chapter about award-winning food books. I love all the works presented here, because they have one thing in common: they make people have an appetite for great food and take readers on a pleasing culinary trip through the different facets of food and international cuisines.

It is a feast for all the senses to immerse in *Seafoodpedia* (p222), designed by Dan Alexander & Co. This book shares seafood recipes, and maritime stories and myths along with enticing, often close-up photographs of different marine animals and textures in an appealing full-bleed layout.

Another visually exciting work is 'For the Love of Stomach' (*Aus Liebe zum Magen*; p230), designed by Studio Mennicke. This book combines excellent cuisine with science via medical explanations of our digestive system. Stories and recipes are enhanced by delicate and minimalist illustrations and finely crafted text. A very successful photographic strategy was also employed to shoot the dishes: double-page, full-bleed spreads show the completed dish on the verso and complementary wines on the recto.

In both of these works, one thing is clear: to present delicious food in its best light, strong conceptual imagery printed large is not a trend, but a must. Aware of this fact, Michelle Ishay-Cohen and Laura Klynstra have also employed an expressive visual language as a strong stylistic device in their beautifully designed books *Heritage* (p244) and *Flavor Flours* (p240). Intense emotional imagery, clever typographical mixes that echo the nature of the content, and generous amounts of white space as a conscious design element make both of these books excellent.

Another design genre is books that focus more on holistic drawing concepts, like 'Culinary Treasures of My Grandmother Ida' (*Le Chicche della Nonna Ida*; p238) by Liuna Virardi and 'Raccoon's Feast' (*Le Festin de Raccoon*; p250) by Marianne Ratier. With simple and skillful strokes and subtle use of colors, Virardi illustrates a tribute to the great and simple Italian cuisine in line with the motto 'less is more'. Ratier's work demonstrates her love of patterns in a lovingly designed book with numerous finely drawn food illustrations for children.

Displaying yet another style, *A Miscellany of Folk Culinary Art* (p234) is one of my personal favorites. In this book, designer Jun Liu opts for a reportage style with the imagery, which fits perfectly with the subject. Although this style decision arose accidentally, Liu succeeds in telling the history of traditional Chinese cuisine with simple and authentic images that convey the essence of this cuisine—simplicity and an affinity with nature—in an ingenious way. The exciting layout, typographic design and well-chosen format make this book a delightful experience.

I hope all of the award-winning books presented in the following pages inspire a great appetite, perhaps even to design your own book. One thing's for sure: there is no lack of subjects for cookbook design, as the projects in this section demonstrate.

Jens Mennicke is an art director, designer, writer and teacher. In 2010 he founded his company Studio Mennicke in Cologne, where he works on visual identities and editorial projects for his business, art and culture clients. His work has received numerous national and international design awards.

Seafoodpedia

- **Design Agency**
  Dan Alexander & Co

- **Size**
  230mm x 310mm

- **Completion**
  2012

- **Photo Credit**
  Clay Mclachlan

- **Awards**
  Gourmand World Cookbook
  Award

Seafoodpedia is a complete guide to fish and seafood that includes recipes, ingredients, and seaside stories. It won first place at the 2013 Gourmand World Cookbook Awards. Dedicated to the geography of the seas and the mythology of marine cuisine, the book charters the ocean's relationship with the kitchen, and culminates with a fantasy story about a voyage of a select few inspired by the sea's siren song.

● עמוד 225: שרימפס קריסטל, ירקות ניסואז, קציפת זיתים
● עמוד 230: אגיולוטי שרימפס

127

לובסטר
Homarus americanus

גמבה (Heb)
Lobster (Eng)
Homard (Fre)
Hummer (Ger)
Astice (It)
Bogavante (Sp)
Американский омар (Rus)

וחושמן של הים, אוכל הכול ואת כולם.
נגיע למעמדים עם דירות אוקינות, כדי שלא יאכל
את הנוספים האחרים במשולת.

● עמוד 215: לובסטר ברייזה

115

114

223

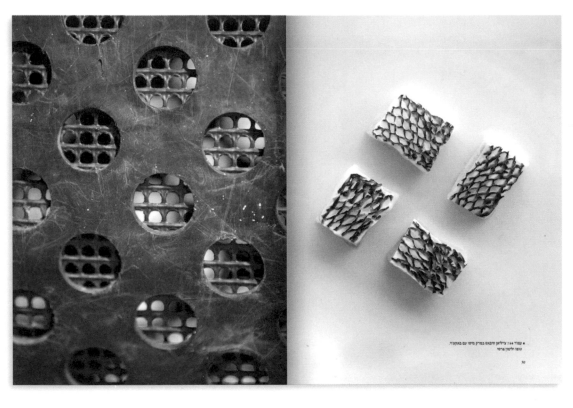

ברבוניה
Mullus surmuletus

מולטס סורמולטוס *(Heb)*
Red Mullet *(Eng)*
Rouget Barbet *(Fr)*
Meerbarbe *(Ger)*
Triglia Di Scoglio *(It)*
Salmonete *(Sp)*
Средиземноморская султанка *(Rus)*

בצרפתית שמו Rouget barbet ופירושו "אדום זקן".
לדג הברבוניה ישנם מחושים אדומים דמויי זקן
בקצה פיו, שבעזרתם הוא סורק את קרקעית הים
כדי למצוא מזון.

● עמ' 59: ברבוניה, אומלטנית, מנוחה מהבריוה בריה.
ריהו נאמות ושלמה ענבניית.

72

ברבוניות אטלנטיות, פסטה בדיו, זיתי טאסוס וסלסה עגבניות

סרדין
Sardina pilchardus

סרדין (Heb)
Sardine (Eng)
Sardine (Fre)
Sardine (Ger)
Sardina (It)
Сардина европейская (Rus)

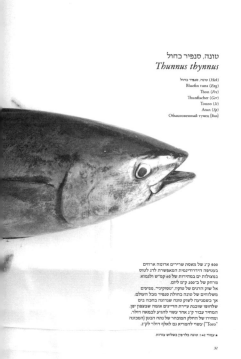

טונה, סנפיר כחול
Thunnus thynnus

טונה, סנפיר כחול (Heb)
Bluefin tuna (Eng)
Thon (Fre)
Thunfischer (Ger)
Tonno (It)
Atún (Sp)
Обыкновенный тунец (Rus)

קארלט
Pleuronectes platessa

שטער אטלנטי (Heb)
Plaice (Eng)
Carrelet (Fre)
Goldbutt (Ger)
Platesa (It)
Solla (Sp)
Морская камбала (Rus)

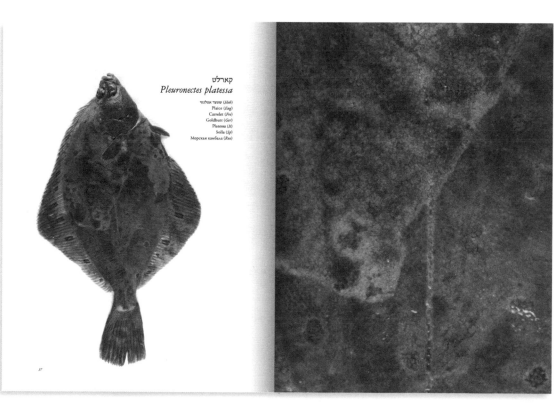

The In Vitro
Meat Cookbook

- **Design Agency**
  Next Nature Network

- **Material**
  Munken Lynx Rough,
  Napura Canvas,
  Napura Pura, Gustav Wasa

- **Size**
  217mm x168mm

- **Completion**
  2014

- **Photo Credit**
  Next Nature Network

- **Awards**
  Dutch Design Research
  Award

Using the format of the cookbook as a storytelling medium, *The In Vitro Meat Cookbook* is a visually stunning exploration of what the new 'food culture' of lab-grown meat might create. This book approaches meat made in this way not just from a design and engineering perspective, but also from a societal and ethical one.

The award-winning cookbook features dozens of recipes that are delicious, uncanny, funny and inspiring: think meat paint, revived dodo wings, meat ice cream, cannibal snacks, steaks knitted like scarves, and see-through sushi, all grown under perfectly controlled conditions. Though the average person can't cook these recipes just yet, they've all been developed with strict culinary rigor.

The delightful and weird recipes are complemented by fascinating interviews and thought-provoking essays from scientists, activists, philosophers and chefs. These experts ensure that the cookbook is as scientifically accurate as possible, all while remaining lively and accessible for a general audience.

115 ← KNITTED MEAT

KNITTED MEAT

While traditional meat cuts refer to the anatomy of the animal — think spare rib, belly slice or T-bone — this is no longer a given with in vitro meat. As a result we can produce meat in any shape our technology and imagination allows us. The knitted meat scenario envisions that 'steaks' will be knitted from thin strains of in vitro meat in any shape and size the customer desires, combining the nostalgia of knitting with the innovative in vitro production technique.

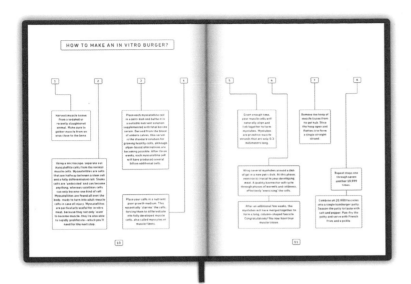

HOW TO MAKE AN IN VITRO BURGER?

POSTBURGER — BLEEDING BURGER

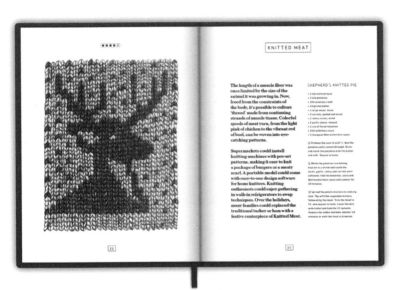

KNITTED MEAT — SHEPHERD'S KNITTED PIE

HOME INCUBATOR — EVERYTHING STEW

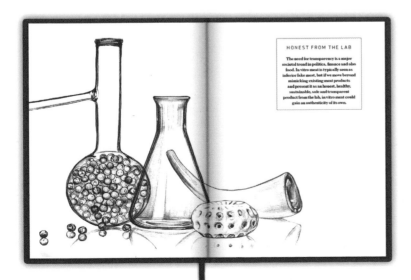

HONEST FROM THE LAB

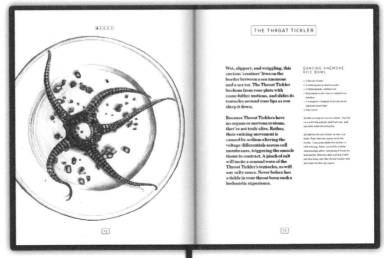

THE THROAT TICKLER — DANCING ANEMONE RICE BOWL

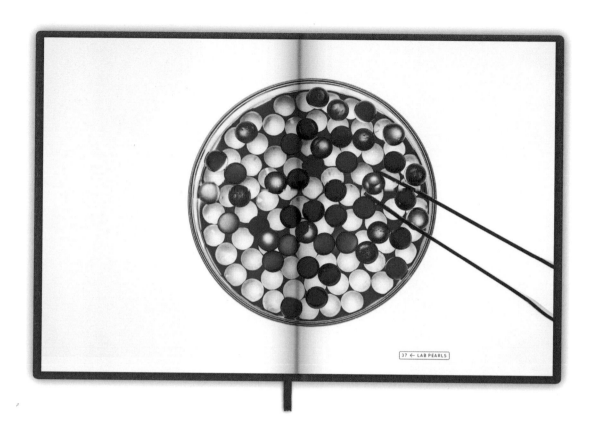

37 ← LAB PEARLS

137 ← MEAT COCKTAIL

Chefs and gastrointestinal experts come together in this book that describes the relationship between the enjoyment of food and what happens to it in our digestive system. Recipes from prominent chefs are paired with complementary wines and scientifically analyzed by a team of doctors.

The book's design combines an innovative photo concept with illustrations and varied typography, all of which aims to whet the reader's appetite. The fonts used are Bodoni, Baskerville, and Univers. The editorial concept was developed by EDLAB—Editorial Development Lab.

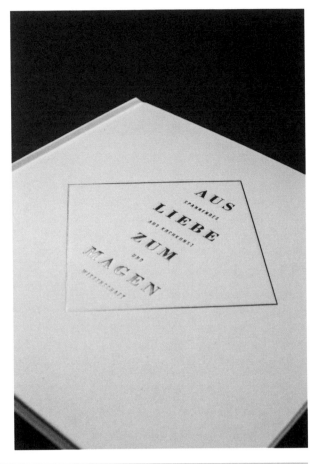

For the Love of Stomach

- **Design Agency**
  Studio Mennicke

- **Designers**
  Jens Mennicke, Markus Olson, Jens Mittelsdorf

- **Material**
  Linen, Coated Paper

- **Printing Technology**
  Hot Foil Stamping

- **Size**
  255mm x 255mm

- **Completion**
  2013

- **Photo Credit**
  Reinhard Hunger

- **Awards**
  Gourmand World Cookbook Award, Winner Germany; Category: Lifestyle, Body & Soul

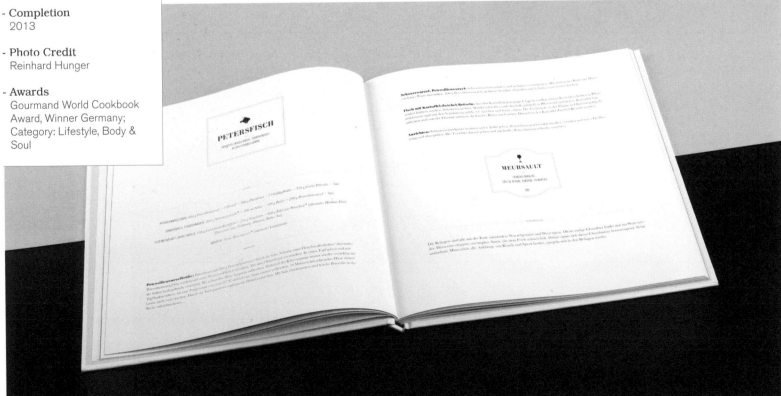

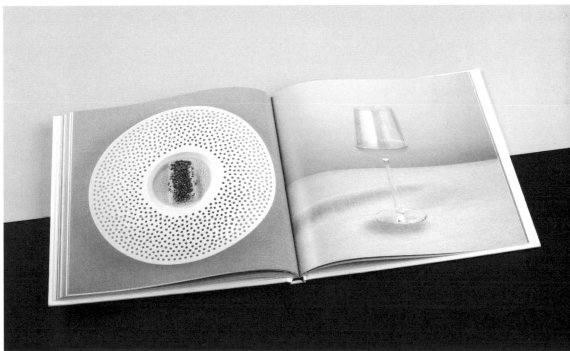

A Miscellany of Folk Culinary Art

- **Designer**
  Jun Liu

- **Size**
  170mm x 240mm

- **Completion**
  2014

- **Awards**
  2013 Gourmand World
  Cookbook Award;
  Category: Chinese Cuisine

A Miscellany of Folk Culinary Art focuses on Chinese menus and food, advocating an attitude of simplicity and affinity with nature. Designer Jun Liu's first cover for the book showed only a white china plate engraved with the name of the book and author, but he decided that it didn't convey the ideas he wanted to communicate, so he came up with another concept. The final cover shows a man holding a traditional iron pot containing a home-style fish and bean curd dish, which better illustrates the book's intention, which was to show how to simply cook good home meals without any chemical additives.

The concept of simplicity is reinforced elsewhere in the book. A visual rhythm is established via picture and text composition, layout design and the use of white space and fine details.

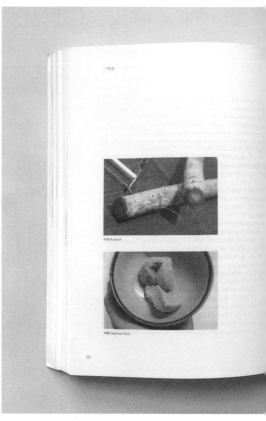

'Culinary Treasures of My Grandmother Ida' (*Le Chicche della Nonna Ida*) is a tribute to Italian grandmothers, carriers of authentic and delicious lifelong recipes, whose commitment and passion in preparation of traditional dishes have positioned Italian cuisine among the most important kinds in the world. This is a cookbook full of fresh products, with specialties ranging from handmade pasta to creamy risottos, revitalizing soups to delicious homemade desserts.

For each recipe, the ingredients and preparation process have been illustrated, and the typography is a handwritten calligraphy. The book is intended to be a sort of notebook, so the illustrations, fonts and colors are executed in a quick and fresh way. Initially the book was going to be produced only in black and white, but designer Liuna Virardi ended up including small touches of color, using only one color for each recipe, which, in some cases, is actually the color that prevails in the dish.

Culinary Treasures of My Grandmother Ida

- **Designer**
  Liuna Virardi

- **Material**
  150gsm Ivory Offset Paper,
  Cardboard Covered with
  90gsm Ivory Offset Paper

- **Size**
  148mm x 210mm

- **Completion**
  2013

- **Photo Credit**
  Piu Martínez

- **Publisher**
  Sd · edicions

- **Awards**
  2013 Gourmand World
  Cookbook Award;
  Category: Best Italian Cuisine
  Book Edited in Spain

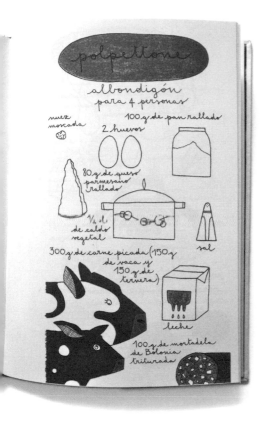

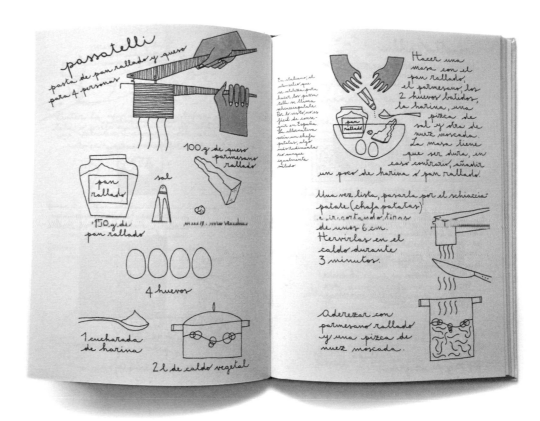

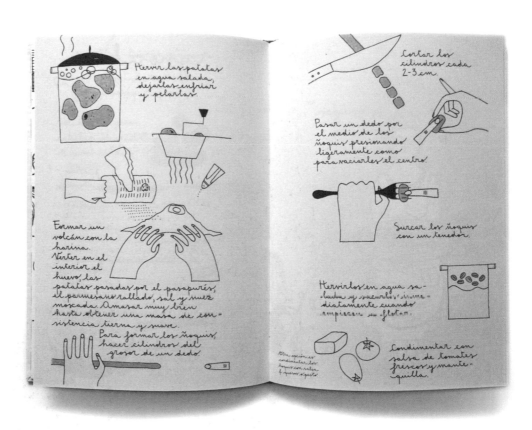

Author Alice Medrich uses flours with flavor to add a new dimension to dessert recipes. Rather than simply add starch and structure to a dessert (as is the case with wheat flour), the flours Medrich cooks with—oat, rice, corn, sorghum, almond, and so on—elevate the taste of the dessert as well. The recipes in this book incorporate the most popular wheat-flour alternatives available today, and use them in interesting ways, both alone and in combination. Chapters are organized by type of flour, each one highlighting the best recipes that flour can be used for—be it muffins, tarts, and scones made with sorghum flour; cakes, cookies, and crumbles made with oat flour; or chocolatey desserts made with teff.

Chapter opener text highlights useful information about each flour: the taste, its flavor affinities, and how it's best used and stored. The design works to highlight these different chapters, so the color scheme reflects the colors of the different flours resulting in a consistent earthy tone throughout. With 125 accessible and delicious recipes, including double oat cookies, buckwheat gingerbread, chocolate chestnut soufflé cake, blueberry corn-flour cobbler, and coconut key lime tart, wheat flour will never be missed.

Flavor Flours
by Alice Medrich

- **Designer**
  Laura Klynstra

- **Material**
  128gsm Matt Art Paper,
  140gsm Wood-Free Paper,
  128gsm Gloss Paper,
  157gsm Glossy Art Paper

- **Printing Technology**
  Matt Lamination, Gold Foil

- **Size**
  189mm x 254mm

- **Completion**
  2014

- **Photo Credit**
  Leigh Beisch

- **Publisher**
  Artisan Books

- **Awards**
  James Beard Foundation
  Award, Best Book of the Year
  in Baking & Desserts

CONTENTS

INTRODUCTION 11

CHAPTER ONE:
RICE FLOUR
51

CHAPTER TWO:
OAT FLOUR
83

CHAPTER THREE:
CORN FLOUR AND CORNMEAL
137

CHAPTER FOUR:
BUCKWHEAT FLOUR
167

CHAPTER FIVE:
CHESTNUT FLOUR
197

CHAPTER SIX:
TEFF FLOUR
229

CHAPTER SEVEN:
SORGHUM FLOUR
261

CHAPTER EIGHT:
NUT AND COCONUT FLOURS
295

CHAPTER NINE: ELEMENTS 333

RESOURCES 351
APPENDIX 354
ACKNOWLEDGMENTS 358
INDEX 359

CHUNKY DOUBLE-CHOCOLATE COCONUT MERINGUES

Add coconut flakes, salted almonds, and chunks of bittersweet and creamy coconut-flavored white chocolate to a light meringue cookie, and you get a riot of creamy, crunchy, chewy, sweet, and salty in every bite. MAKES 45 TO 50 COOKIES

1 cup (140 grams) roasted salted almonds, coarsely chopped

4 ounces (115 grams) 70% chocolate, cut into chunks, or ⅔ cup purchased chocolate chunks or chips

1 cup (40 grams) unsweetened dried flaked coconut (coconut chips)

2 ounces (60 grams) coconut white chocolate (such as Lindt), cut into ½-inch squares

3 large egg whites, at room temperature

¼ teaspoon cream of tartar

½ cup plus 2 tablespoons (125 grams) sugar

EQUIPMENT

Stand mixer with whisk attachment or handheld mixer

2 baking sheets, lined with parchment paper

Position racks in the upper and lower thirds of the oven and preheat the oven to 200°F.

In a small bowl, combine one-quarter of the almonds, dark chocolate, and coconut for sprinkling. Set aside.

In a medium bowl, mix the remaining almonds, chocolate, and coconut with the coconut white chocolate. Set aside.

Combine the egg whites and cream of tartar in the bowl of the stand mixer (or in a large bowl if using a handheld mixer). Beat on medium-high speed (or on high speed with the handheld mixer) until the egg whites are creamy white (instead of translucent) and hold a soft shape when the beaters are lifted. Continue to beat on medium to high speed, adding the sugar a little at a time, for 1½ to 2 minutes, until the egg whites are very stiff and have a dull sheen. Use a large rubber spatula to fold in the mixture of nuts, coconut, and both chocolates, just until blended.

Drop generous tablespoons of meringue 1½ inches apart on the lined baking sheets. Make sure all of the batter fits on the two sheets so all can be baked at once; if necessary, make each cookie a little bigger. Sprinkle the meringues with the reserved chocolate, almonds, and coconut.

Bake for 1½ hours, rotating the pans from top to bottom and from front to back halfway through the baking time to ensure even baking. Remove a test meringue and let it cool completely before taking a bite (meringues are never crisp when hot). If the test meringue is completely dry and crisp, turn off the oven and let the remaining meringues cool completely in the oven. If the test meringue is soft or chewy or sticks to your teeth, bake for another 15 to 30 minutes before cooling in the oven.

To prevent cookies from becoming sticky, put them in an airtight container as soon as they are cool. Cookies keep for at least 2 weeks.

CHESTNUTS were a critically important food in Europe and Asia

long before the cultivation of wheat or potatoes. European settlers found an abundance of the trees on American shores too, dispersed over 200 million acres of eastern woodland, the length of the eastern seaboard, and as far west as the Mississippi. Like their Asian and European counterparts, Native Americans subsisted on chestnuts, raw or roasted, in gruels and stews, and pounded into meal to make unleavened breads, and the new settlers followed suit. Chestnuts might be a staple of our diet today had not a lethal blight wiped out an estimated 4 billion trees—one-quarter of the hardwood forest—in the first half of the twentieth century.

Historical reliance on chestnuts as a subsistence food—and even their use in modern welfare Europe when grain crops and milled flour were scarce—branded chestnuts as the food of the poor. Even today, chestnut trees are called "bread trees" in parts of southern Europe where chestnut flour is still widely used to make bread.

But in affluent countries, especially in urban centers, the food of the poor becomes chic. Chestnuts have become a celebration food. We savor them roasted from carts on snowy street corners and stuff them into holiday birds. Candied chestnuts, chestnut cream, chestnuts in syrup, chestnut honey, and canned cooked steamed chestnuts are luxe items sold in gourmet shops where, with luck, you might also find chestnut flour.

Chestnut flour is milled from pulverized dried chestnuts and has a soft starchy texture and a tendency to clump, similar to oat flour. Unlike most nut flours, chestnut flour is about 78 percent carbohydrates and only 1 percent fat. It varies in color from pale to warm tan—sometimes related to whether the flour is raw or roasted—and has a sweet aroma and a sweet, slightly nutty flavor. Raw and roasted flours are interchangeable in recipes, but I prefer the flavor of raw flour. Either way, beware of flour that smells and tastes excessively smoky. It is traditional in Italy to dry the nuts over a wood fire, but the flavor of some flours produced this way is decidedly tainted by too much smoke. For desserts, especially, you'll want to use flour with little if any smoky flavor.

Chestnut flour gives cakes a very soft crumb that is never gritty and has plenty of flavor. It can be used alone, without any other flour, and it works wonderfully in all kinds of sponge and egg-based cakes, meringues, and a simple honey pudding. Paired with rice flour, it makes a flavorful shortbread crust for tarts (see page 209) and festive quince-filled cookies (see page 223)

FLAVOR AFFINITIES FOR CHESTNUT FLOUR

Honey (especially chestnut honey), hazelnuts, walnuts, pine nuts, dark or white chocolate, brandy or cognac, Grand Marnier, sweet fortified wine such as sherry or marsala, caramel, cardamom, fresh cheese such as ricotta, mascarpone cheese, crème fraîche, cinnamon, coffee, figs, ginger, maple, prunes and plums, pears, apples, orange zest, brown sugar

WHERE TO BUY AND HOW TO STORE

Chestnut flour is available in some better supermarkets and specialty stores, sometimes only during the fall holidays. It is otherwise available by mail order, year round. If you are not using it up within 2 to 3 months, keep chestnut flour in an airtight container in the refrigerator or freezer. See Resources (page 351) for my preferred source.

RICE
FLOUR

from the dough; just press very gently all over to adhere the dough and fruit. Put the baking sheet in the fridge and refrigerate for at least 2 hours but preferably overnight.

Position racks in the upper and lower thirds of the oven and preheat the oven to 325°F.

Remove the dough from the refrigerator and peel the paper from the top. Dust the top of the dough and a cutting board very lightly with rice flour. Lift the parchment under the dough, flip the dough over onto the cutting board, and peel off the paper. Sprinkle with the coarse sugar and pat lightly to make sure the sugar adheres. Use a heavy knife to trim the edges. Use a straight-down "guillotine" stroke to cut 5 strips and then cut each strip into 5 pieces to make 25 pieces. Don't worry if the dough cracks when you cut it. Use a spatula to lift and place the cookies 1 inch apart on the lined pans.

Bake for 15 to 20 minutes, until the cookies are golden brown at the edges and deep golden brown when you peek underneath (carefully, as the cookies are very fragile while hot). Rotate the pans from front to back and top to bottom a little over halfway through the baking. Place the pans on racks, or slide the liners from the pans onto racks to cool. Cool the cookies completely before stacking or storing. Cookies may be kept for at least a week in an airtight container.

SORGHUM FLOUR | 287

Heritage
by Sean Brock

- **Designer**
  Michelle Ishay-Cohen

- **Material**
  128gsm Matt Art Paper,
  140gsm Wood-Free Paper,
  White Arlin, 157gsm Glossy
  Art Paper

- **Printing Technology**
  Foil Stamping, Varnish,
  Scuff-Free Matt Lamination

- **Size**
  213mm x 289mm

- **Completion**
  2014 .

- **Photo Credit**
  Peter Frank Edwards

- **Publisher**
  Artisan Books

- **Awards**
  James Beard Foundation
  Award, Best Book of the Year
  in American Cooking; IACP
  Julia Child First Book Award

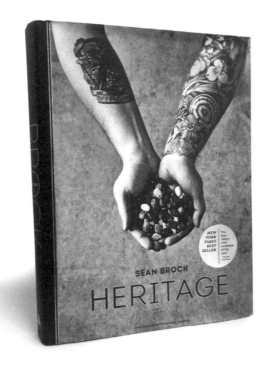

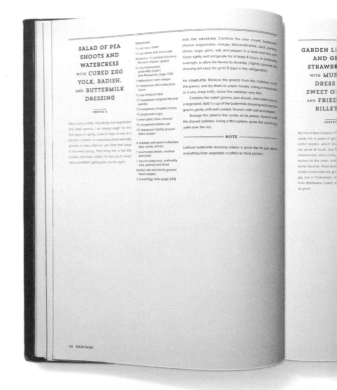

Award-winning American chef Sean Brock cooks dishes that are driven by heritage ingredients and that reinterpret the flavors of his youth in Appalachia and of his adopted hometown of Charleston, while also embracing the influences of his global travels. In this book, he shares his favorite recipes for both the sophisticated dishes that he serves in his restaurants and the totally relatable foods that he cooks at home.

The design objective was to create an elegant, masculine cookbook. It was important that the look was timeless but also contained some flair from old cookbooks. Recipes are laid out in a three-column grid with an aged-looking ruled line at the top to anchor everything. The grid allows many of the recipes to fit onto one page and provides plenty of white space, which draws the eye in and makes the recipes look less intimidating. It was important to make this book very accessible to a large audience, so the designer selected airy typefaces that make even long complicated recipes not look too dense.

SLOW-COOKED LAMB RACK with SPRING FAVAS, MALTED BARLEY, and ROASTED CHANTERELLES

SERVES 4

THE PASTURE 153

WILD-RAMP-AND-CRAB-STUFFED HUSHPUPPIES with GREEN GODDESS DRESSING

78 HERITAGE

CHICKEN
SIMPLY ROASTED
IN A SKILLET

SERVES 2
HUNGRY PEOPLE

I love cooking chicken like this at home. It fills the house with an amazing aroma. The flavors of garlic, lemon, and parsley are classic and simply delicious. You can throw the dish together at the last minute with minimal shopping and prep. I serve it with a simple salad or a very fresh vegetable quickly cooked on the side.

GARLIC CONFIT

6 large garlic cloves, peeled
1 teaspoon sugar
1 tablespoon kosher salt
1 teaspoon freshly cracked black pepper
2 tablespoons extra-virgin olive oil

CHICKEN

1 whole chicken (about 3 pounds)
Kosher salt and freshly cracked black pepper
½ cup canola oil

PAN SAUCE

2 cups Chicken Stock (page 319)
1 tablespoon all-purpose flour
1 cup flat-leaf parsley leaves cut into very thin strips
Grated zest and juice of 1 lemon

FOR THE GARLIC CONFIT: Preheat the oven to 400°F. Cut two 12-inch squares of aluminum foil and lay one piece on top of the other. Place the garlic cloves on the foil. Sprinkle with the sugar, salt, and pepper. Pour the olive oil over the garlic cloves. Shape the foil into a pouch by bringing the edges of the foil together over the garlic and sealing them. Flatten the bottom of the pouch so it will stay upright in the oven and place it on a baking sheet.

Roast the garlic for about 30 minutes, until the cloves are very soft but not falling apart. Set the garlic aside in the pouch. Leave the oven on.

MEANWHILE, FOR THE CHICKEN: Using kitchen shears, cut down along both sides of the backbone, then clip it out. Cut the wings off at the first joint. (Reserve the backbone and wing tips to make stock.) Split the chicken in half. Use paper towels to dry the skin. Season both sides of the chicken with salt and pepper. Place the chicken in a baking dish and let it sit at room temperature for 20 minutes.

Place two 12-inch cast-iron skillets over high heat. When the skillets smoke, add ¼ cup of the canola oil to each. As soon as the oil smokes, carefully add a half chicken to each skillet, skin side down. Weight each chicken half with another heavy skillet or pan so it stays flat and browns evenly. Cook the chicken, with the weights on it, until the skin is crispy and evenly browned, 5 to 7 minutes. Remove the weights.

Flip the chicken over, and place the skillets in the oven. Roast the chicken for about 20 minutes, until an instant-read thermometer inserted into the thickest part of the thigh reads 155°F. Place the chicken on plates to rest while you make the sauce.

FOR THE PAN SAUCE: Combine the roasting juices and fats from both skillets into one; set aside. Place the other skillet on the stove over medium heat until it is hot to the touch, about 1 minute. Pour 1 cup of the chicken stock into the skillet and use a spatula to scrape the browned bits from the bottom of the skillet, then gently boil the stock to reduce it by half, about 5 minutes. Add the remaining cup of stock and set aside.

Place the skillet with the roasting juices over medium heat. Sprinkle the flour evenly over the juices and gently whisk it in until there are no lumps. Reduce the heat to low and cook for 2 minutes, stirring constantly with the whisk; do not let the roux get too dark around the edge. Whisk in the chicken stock, making sure to fully emulsify it. Increase the heat to high and bring the sauce to a simmer, then reduce the heat to medium-high and reduce the sauce until it coats the back of a spoon, about 5 minutes.

Add the parsley, lemon zest and juice, and 2 tablespoons of the garlic oil from the pouch of garlic and whisk to combine.

TO COMPLETE: Place the garlic and pan sauce over the chicken and enjoy.

247

From Garden, Forest, and Treats

- **Designer**
  Agata Królak

- **Material**
  Jacket: 350gsm Paper High Brightness;
  Text: 200gsm Paper High Brightness

- **Size**
  210mm x 210mm

- **Completion**
  2013

- **Photo Credit**
  Agata Królak

- **Publisher**
  Wydawnictwo Dwie Siostry

- **Awards**
  Trójkowy Znak Jakości, Polish Radio Quality Trademark, 2014

This Polish cookbook contains 73 recipes gathered from the author's friends and family along with old family photographs. The book is divided into three parts: dishes made from ingredients in your garden (fruits, weeds, vegetables, and so on); dishes made from forest ingredients (weeds, wild berries, nuts); and dishes from fruits and vegetables found at the market (ones that are less popular in home gardens and farms but still delicious and healthy). Each part has four categories: snacks, spreads (such as jams, pastes, and pickles), nonalcoholic drinks, and liqueurs.

The design of the book, from the double-square spreads and handwritten text to the black-and-white photographs and childlike illustrations, was meant to be friendly, familiar, and most of all sentimental, since the recipes are often from the contributors' childhoods, passed on from their mothers and grandmothers.

While the layout of the book might, at first sight, seem frivolous, it is intentionally neat and simple. Each spread contains a handwritten recipe, page number, and color band (to indicate which part of the book you're in) on the left, and an illustration on the right. Dishes are presented as playful, hand-drawn pictures rather than photographs to encourage readers to experiment and have fun while making the recipes. All of the illustrations are presented as a pantry shelf filled with the results of each recipe, for example, jars of pickles.

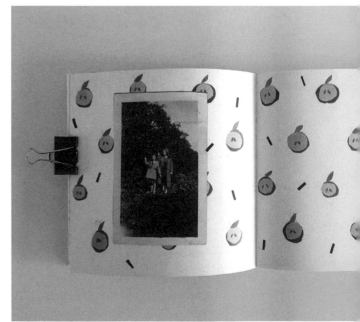

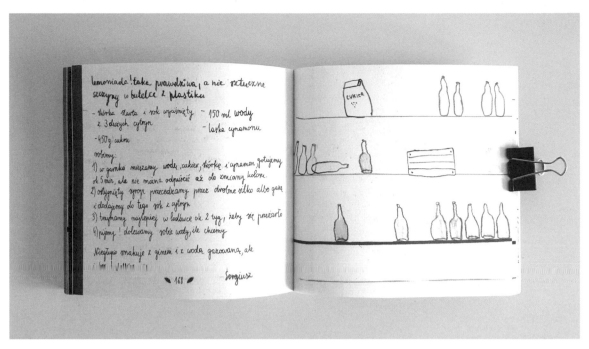

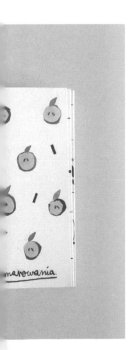

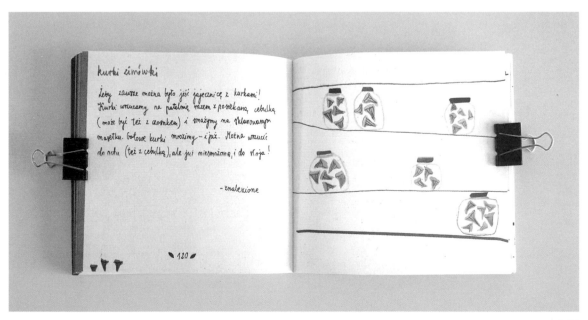

Raccoon's Feast

- **Designer**
  Marianne Ratier

- **Material**
  Matt Coated Paper

- **Size**
  240mm x 320mm

- **Completion**
  2014

- **Photo Credit**
  Marianne Ratier

- **Publisher**
  Marmaille et Compagnie

- **Awards**
  Gourmand World Cookbook
  Award 2014

'Raccoon's Feast' (*Le Festin de Raccoon*) was not initially intended to be a book. It all started with an exhibition in a Parisian restaurant named Barbershop in October 2012, when Marianne Ratier decided to reinterpret 10 of the restaurant's dishes as illustrated wallpapers, offering an interesting take on the menu. She has had a passion for drawing repetitive patterns—which naturally lend themselves to a wallpaper design—since childhood, and these patterns feature in the Barbershop illustrations. While repetition can look boring, Ratier knew how to avoid falling into that trap: any mechanical repetition in her illustrations was broken by a raccoon! A few months later, a young editor from Marmaille et Compagnie suggested compiling Ratier's illustrations into a *Where's Wally?*—type children's food book, where both the raccoon and ingredients from the dishes are hidden among different designs.

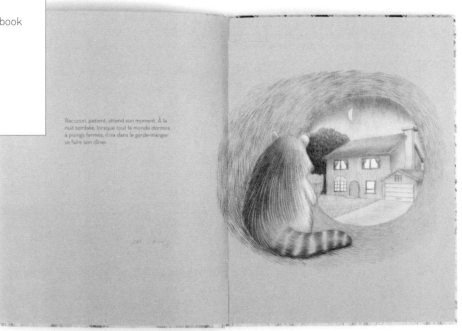

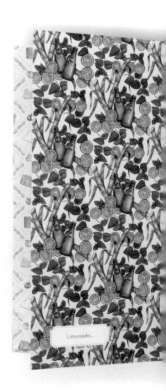

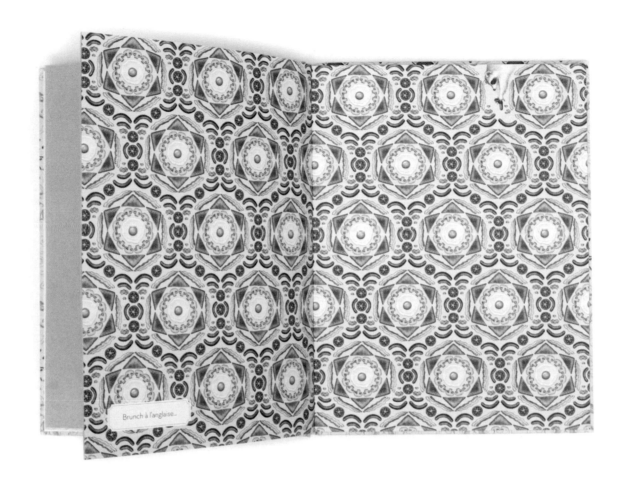

Brunch à l'anglaise...

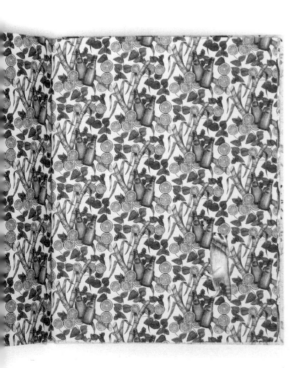

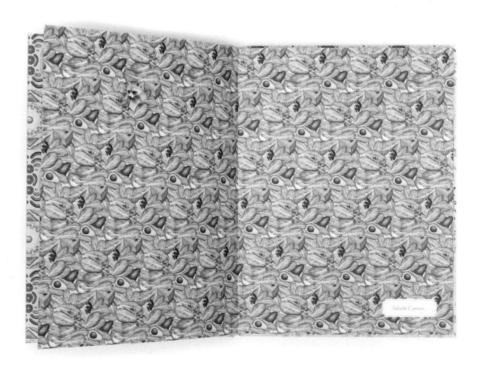

Galette Comtoise...

Punch
aux épices

RHUM
LIQUEUR DE BANANE
JUS DE CITRON VERT
ORANGES PRESSÉES
CANNELLE
GIROFLE
MUSCADE
POIVRE
———

Cheesecake

VANILLE
SPÉCULOOS
CREAM CHEESE
CRÈME FOUETTÉE
SUCRE
COULIS DE FRUITS ROUGES
———

Cheese
burger

STEAK
SALADE
OIGNONS
PICKLES
CHEDDAR FONDU
COLESLAW
FRITES
———

Fondant
au chocolat

CHOCOLAT
ŒUFS
SUCRE
BEURRE
FARINE
BANANES
COCO GUANABANA
———

Les invités sont arrivés, les voitures se garent dans l'allée. Raccoon se frotte les yeux, déconfit... À force de surveiller, il s'était endormi.

Brunch, salade, saumon... Toutes ces bonnes choses n'étaient qu'un rêve ! Dépité, il regarde les convives se régaler de ces mets qu'il aurait tant voulu goûter.

Brunch
à l'Anglaise

ŒUFS AU PLAT
BACON
SAUCISSES
HARICOTS À LA TOMATE
CHAMPIGNONS
TOMATES RÔTIES
TOASTS
—

Salade
Caesar

ROMAINE
FILET DE POULET GRILLÉ
AVOCAT
ŒUF POCHÉ
PARMESAN
CROÛTONS
SAUCE CAESAR
—

Saumon
sauce Chien

SAUMON
OIGNONS CIVES
TOMATES
OIGNONS
GOUSSES D'AIL
BRANCHES DE PERSIL
CITRON
—

Tartare
de Bœuf

BŒUF
CORNICHONS
MOUTARDE
KETCHUP
OIGNONS
ÉCHALOTES
PERSIL
CORIANDRE
CIBOULETTE
ŒUF
—

INDEX

Published in Australia in 2016 by
The Images Publishing Group Pty Ltd
Shanghai Office
ABN 89 059 734 431
6 Bastow Place, Mulgrave, Victoria 3170, Australia
Tel: +61 3 9561 5544 Fax: +61 3 9561 4860
books@imagespublishing.com
www.imagespublishing.com

Title: Delicious Book Design
Author: Megan van Staden (ed.)
ISBN: 9781864706550 (hardback)

For Catalogue-in-Publication data, please see the National Library of Australia entry

Printed by Toppan Leefung Printing (Shenzhen) Co. Ltd / China